Today's Learners, Tomorrow's Leaders

INSPIRE YOUR STUDENTS TO SUCCEED IN SCHOOL AND BEYOND

Tisha Poncio and Rick Butterworth

International Society for Technology in Education
ARLINGTON, VIRGINIA

Today's Learners, Tomorrow's Leaders
Inspire Your Students to Succeed in School and Beyond
Tisha Poncio and Rick Butterworth

Director of Books and Journals: *Emily Reed*
Senior Acquisitions Editor: *Valerie Witte*
Developmental and Copy Editor: *Linda Laflamme*
Proofreader: *Joanna Szabo*
Indexer: *Valerie Haynes Perry*
Book Design and Production: *Danielle Foster*
Cover Design: *Edwin Ouellette*

Library of Congress Cataloging-in-Publication Data
Names: Poncio, Tisha, author. | Butterworth, Rick, author.
Title: Today's learners, tomorrow's leaders : inspire your students to succeed in school and beyond / Tisha Poncio and Rick Butterworth.
Description: First edition. | Arlington, Virginia : International Society for Technology in Education, [2025] | Includes bibliographical references and index.
Identifiers: LCCN 2025000638 (print) | LCCN 2025000639 (ebook) | ISBN 9798888370476 (paperback) | ISBN 9798888370452 (epub) | ISBN 9798888370469 (pdf)
Subjects: LCSH: Leadership--Study and teaching. | Entrepreneurship--Study and teaching. | Problem solving. | Life skills.
Classification: LCC HD57.7 .P655 2025 (print) | LCC HD57.7 (ebook) | DDC 650.1071/2--dc23/eng/20250217
LC record available at https://lccn.loc.gov/2025000638
LC ebook record available at https://lccn.loc.gov/2025000639

First Edition

ISBN: 979-8-88837-047-6
Ebook version available

Printed in the United States of America
ISTE® is a registered trademark of the International Society for Technology in Education.

About ISTE

The International Society for Technology in Education (ISTE) is a nonprofit that brings together a passionate community of global educators. Our vision is that all students engage in transformative learning experiences that spark their imagination and prepare them to thrive in learning and life. ISTE's mission is to empower educators to reimagine and redesign learning through impactful pedagogy and meaningful technology use. We achieve this by offering transformative professional learning, fostering vibrant communities, and ensuring that digital tools and experiences are accessible and effective.

Related ISTE Titles

Digital Citizenship in Action, Second Edition: Empowering Students to Engage in Online Communities
By Kristen Mattson

Chart a New Course: A Guide to Teaching Essential Skills for Tomorrow's World
By Rachelle Dené Poth

To see all books available from ISTE, please visit iste.org/books.

About the Authors

Tisha Poncio received her MS in Learning Technologies from the University of North Texas in 2019 to expand her passion to inspire learners, educators, and leaders. With over two decades of dedicated service in the education and instructional design fields, Tisha's energy and enthusiasm have fueled her success as a teacher, digital learning coach, learner, and leader. Throughout her career, Tisha has left a lasting impact on her students, guiding them in subjects ranging from web design, graphic design, business computers, programming to English, broadcast journalism, and entrepreneurship. In addition to her exceptional work as a classroom teacher, she served as an innovative digital learning specialist for more than twelve years, leading and inspiring fellow educators and administrators with meaningful technology integration and instructional design that supports all learners. Tisha's commitment to staying at the forefront of educational and emerging technologies is evident throughout her journey. She was named a TCEA (Texas Computer Education Association) finalist for the Instructional Technology Specialist of the Year award in 2018 and contributed a chapter to *EduMatch 2020 Snapshot in Education: Remote Learning Edition*. She continues seeking opportunities that support and empower students, teachers, and leaders.

Rick Butterworth is a founder, product designer, and developer who has dedicated nearly two decades to revolutionizing user interactions and learning experiences in online applications. With a strong background in UX/UI, front-end development, and product management, Rick possesses a versatile skill set that drives innovation and creates meaningful impact. Rick's journey began at the University of Salford, where he cultivated Visual Basic Script and aviation technology skills. Overcoming dyslexia, he embraced his unique learning style, which ultimately fueled his determination to succeed and help learners who struggle with their learning challenges. In his early twenties, Rick began his entrepreneurship by looking for a solution to a problem and developing his first software application, which is used by aviation enthusiasts. He then founded a successful web design and development company catering to such diverse industries as technology, aviation, photography, and media. Additionally, his expertise encompasses wireframing, prototyping, and interactive design, as well as HTML, CSS, JavaScript, PHP, and React programming languages.

Acknowledgments

Author Acknowledgments

We express heartfelt gratitude to the many contributors who made this book possible.

To the student contributors—Julianna Parsons, Douglas Palmer, Avery Davenport, Annora Elias, Jace, and many others—thank you for your insights, enthusiasm, and courage to share your voices to shape the foundation of this work.

To the incredible educator contributors—Stacie White, Michelle Adkins, Laura Steinbrink, and Rachel Medrano—thank you for your dedication to student success and inspiring innovation in education and your classrooms.

To Mark Perez and Wilborn Blalock, thank you for sharing your industry perspectives, which added real-world applications and valuable insights.

To our ISTE peer reviewers and editors—Valerie Witte and Linda Laflamme—your feedback, knowledge, patience, and leadership have been invaluable throughout the writing and editing process.

To Cody Holt, Executive Director of Learning Technologies, thank you for opening the doors to your forward-thinking classroom which sparked the idea to give students a deeper experience connecting the classroom to careers.

To those in the educational technology space who have shared their expertise, supported us, and challenged us to think of teaching and learning differently than we were taught, you continue to inspire us with your social posts, books, videos, knowledge, personal passions, and stories.

To the students who joined in the audacious idea of a student-led classroom and leadership movement, your willingness to innovate, support, and lead exceeded all expectations. Special thanks to Juliana Parsons, Annora Elias, Jillian Parsons, Jared Weaver, Milena Carlson, Blake Stogner, Brady Poche, Conner Sanders, Avery Camp, Erin Camp, Wyatt Smith, Ellie Lykins, Olivia Snyder, Nathaniel Matthews, Judith Matehuala, Charity Mpofu, Liam Baksa, and so many others.

For our fellow neurodiverse learners and leaders: We implemented the same strategies and practices in this book as we worked through writing, editing, peer feedback, and self-reflection. Behind every page and resource were many early mornings, late nights, sweat, tears, passion, and hopefully some inspiration to remind you that nothing is impossible and you *are* a leader. Your creativity and resilience inspire us daily. This work is a testament to the power of diverse minds coming together to create meaningful change in education and beyond.

Publisher's Acknowledgments

ISTE gratefully acknowledges the contributions of the following:

ISTE Standards reviewers	Manuscript reviewers
Mary Beth Clifton	Salenah Cartier
Michelle Eckler	Stacy Hawthorne
	Bonnie Nieves
	Emily Thomas

Dedication

For Mrs. Ann Elam and all educators who embody her dedication to students: You knew I was meant to shine long before I did. Though I lacked confidence in my abilities, talents, and knowledge, you saw my potential and nurtured my natural ability for communication and expression. Though we spent only a year together, you quietly saved me and finally gave me the confidence and permission to use my voice. Your empowerment then has made this book possible now. Forever grateful, thank you.

—Tisha

For all those navigating dyslexia: In the moments you feel you are not "good enough," not capable of achieving the things you love or are passionate about because you believe you are "not smart" or "not clever," remember this: Focus on your strengths, as they are your greatest asset because they are distinctly different from those around you. They will give you the ability to do what everyone else can do *and* surpass your own expectations.

—Rick

Contents

CHAPTER 3 Every Learner Is a Leader 23

CHAPTER 4 Student Entrepreneurship 43

CHAPTER 5 Promoting Problem-Solving with Students . . . 59

Preface

Tisha was given the opportunity to combine two passions in her role as a digital learning coach: empowering educators to integrate technology in a meaningful way and providing a learning environment for students to discover, acknowledge, and lean into their potential as learners, creators, and entrepreneurs. This allowed her to view learning environments, student potential, and her teaching practice in a completely new way. By stepping into a true facilitator role, she gave her students room to learn outside of a traditional teaching environment with real-world scenarios and creative solutions. They became autonomous and motivated to share their learning experiences with audiences outside of the classroom and were empowered to launch their own branding and businesses. Students also created their own version of a student-led podcast, which they presented to global audiences, sharing the power of digital portfolios, digital citizenship, and student leadership.

While Tisha was gathering experience in the classroom, Rick was unknowingly beginning his entrepreneurial journey. Coding and problem-solving were the seeds that began to grow his interest in entrepreneurship. Rather than continuing his aviation studies, he found a love for and fulfillment in creating things through code. He discovered that self-paced learning and autonomy served him in a way that traditional learning did not. Following this career path, he started his own company, became a consultant, and co-founded an educational technology start-up.

During this time, Tisha and Rick crossed paths and discovered they both have a shared dedication to emerging technologies, forward-thinking in education, and accessibility for all learners. Despite having to confront their learning challenges—Tisha with ADHD and Rick with dyslexia—they shared a vision to break barriers and level the playing field for all learners. This began their collaborative journey, fueled by their passion and understanding of the obstacles they faced, as they realized learning challenges possess a superpower that allows for creative problem-solving, intuitive decision-making, pattern recognition, outside-of-the-box thinking, spatial awareness, and a drive for entrepreneurship (Hollings-Tennant, 2021, discusses these in detail).

Introduction

What is the origin of a classroom, what influenced its creation, and how can we create more inclusive, supportive, and motivational environments for all students? These are just some of the many questions that we (Tisha and Rick) think about as we strive to evolve classrooms to strengthen every student's path toward a better and brighter future. The goal of this book is to support that move.

Let us borrow H. G. Wells's Time Machine and journey back to the early 19th century when the *Bell-Lancasterian Principle*, also called the *Monitorial Method*, was introduced in the northeastern parts of America's education system. This method of teaching was very different from what we have today. Students of all ages would gather in a large room with a single teacher teaching a lesson to a select number of students or monitors who would then teach their classes and impart the lessons to other students (Blakemore, 2023).

The Monitorial Method received significant resistance from parents because they felt their students were spending more time teaching than learning, which enforced the mindset that students could not learn from each other. It was replaced around 1840 with the *Prussian Model*, introduced by Horace Mann after he discovered it during his travels in Europe. He introduced it to the Massachusetts Board of Education, and they approved and implemented the classroom design you still see today: students grouped by age with chairs facing the same direction in rows and columns with the teacher at the front of the room (Blakemore, 2023).

Associated with "discipline, obedience, conformity, rigid curriculum, mindless memorization, [and] suppression of creativity," the Prussian Model reflects the "factory model of education": buckets, assembly lines, age-based cohorts, whole-class instruction, and standardization (Watters, 2015). This teacher-centered model dedicated to specific age groups forms an environment of control, discipline, and assumption. Students are expected to learn in a controlled manner, waiting for the teacher—the holder of information—to share knowledge before students prove competency of skills and move up in grade or subject matter.

Although the Prussian Model remained the primary classroom structure, over the next 180 years education evolved steadily. Mandatory education for all students was implemented, and in the 1890s the Committee of Ten was created to work toward standardization of education across the U.S. (Weidner, n.d.). The 1960s ushered in desegregation. In the 1990s, broader access to the internet and technology integration meant information became far easier to access than ever before. STEM (Science, Technologies, Engineering, and Math) and STEAM (Science, Technologies, Engineering, Arts, and Math) gained significant traction in the early 2000s, and accessibility to technologies became a more significant requirement for those with learning challenges (National Center for Education Statistics, 2003).

Progress and Challenges

The educational strides over the last two centuries have paved the way for a more inclusive, diverse, and accessible modern-day classroom. Still, one piece of the proverbial puzzle sticks out. Much like in the 1840s, there is still a mindset that students' autonomy and collaboration cannot coincide with a teacher dictating the learning. The foundation and basic structures of classrooms have not changed much since Mann first introduced the Prussian Model to the U.S. education system. Efficiency and standardized learning and assessments reign supreme over individuality, performance-based assessments, student-led learning, creativity, problem-solving, and more. On the surface, today's "technological revolution" appears to be advancing learners and their skills. However, preparing students for their future requires us all to review our beliefs, perspectives, and practices to support transformational learning and create spaces that empower learners to become impactful leaders.

As newly hired teachers, we all entered classrooms with ideas, inspiration, and creativity. Our passions to change the world through teaching was the motivation for us to join the profession. Over time, however, we began to see glimpses of a system that continues to limit and restrict us from revolutionizing the classroom experience. As with any change in structure or process, there is resistance. Some teachers find comfort in the idea that "this is how we have always done it" and safety in knowing that they have adapted over time to a comfortable routine. That same routine, however, also denies us the ability to grow and steals opportunities for critical thinking, collaboration, and curiosity. Comfort does not create leaders, innovators, or entrepreneurs. If we do not change and grow, students will become by-products of our current behaviors and we will leave a legacy that has changed nothing and continues to repeat itself.

Our aim for this book is to show that learning is not linear and that the students entering classrooms are as unique as their fingerprints. Leading them to success in the classroom and beyond does not demand more time; it only requires pausing to see students for who they truly are. What sparks their creativity? What piques their interests? What prompts them to stand out academically and as their authentic selves?

If you are looking for simple and easy ideas, inspiration, and strategies to grow young leaders, you are in the right place. This book was written with no rules or set sequence so that the reading and learning can mold itself to your unique preferences and needs. For example, you might introduce problem-solving (Chapter 5) to students the first month of instruction, and then later begin implementing entrepreneurship (Chapter 4). Similarly, we have chosen not to highlight any particular digital products because it is our core belief that pedagogy and instructional strategies must come first. Integrating technology and weaving it into projects and assignments should be intentional and should support students with individualized learning and accessibility, as well as help them make connections that would not otherwise be possible.

About This Book

We (Tisha and Rick) discovered quickly that we have similar values, goals, and purpose and that we experienced similar frustrations, pain points, and challenges as young learners. Like many of you, we realized quickly that our experiences in school did not favor how we learn best, and, therefore, it took us much longer to realize and learn how to accommodate for our way of thinking, leading, and growing. Our motivation for this book is to show the possibilities when students and educators are given the room and freedom to be curious, to create, and to see themselves as successful beyond any limitations placed upon them by others. To truly model the value of this book, we put into practice the same strategies we have written about. Working in this way ensured our effectiveness with intentional collaboration, room for creative ideas, experiences with leading and following, and, most importantly, time for feedback and constructive discourse.

ISTE Standards and Transformational Learning Principles

To avoid unfamiliarity or duplication of content, each chapter was led by one of us, with the other reviewing, editing, and discussing the final content. All chapters align with the ISTE+ASCD Transformational Learning Principles (TLPs), as well as the ISTE Standards for Students and Educators. We will list the key connections at the start of each chapter. In addition, where appropriate, we include connections to the principles and standards that correspond with strategies you can implement with students, to support them in developing their strengths around leadership.

iste.org/Standards   tinyurl.com/iste-TLP

Scan the QR codes to view the ISTE Standards and TLPs in full.

Transformative Success Strategies

Throughout this book, you will discover strategies and actionable ideas to help students apply and engage with the topics explored in each chapter. The strategies provided are closely aligned with the ISTE+ASCD Transformational Learning Principles and the ISTE Standards, offering educators effective methods designed to cultivate leadership and entrepreneurial mindsets. Look out for these icons (▶▶▶) to cue you to keep an eye out for these practical tips.

Voices Driving Change

Additionally, you will hear from students, teachers, and entrepreneurs throughout the book. We wanted to give each individual a space to express their voice, share experiences inside the classroom, and offer insights into the skills they learned after graduation that future leaders need.

Transformational Playbook of Resources

At the end of each chapter, you'll find a QR code that leads to a dedicated space with additional materials. The resources provided reinforce the ideas in each chapter and include templates for you to download and adapt, images for you to review, and other instructional resources that will help guide and support you to lead and transform your classroom.

Chapter Roadmap

To help you decide where to start, here's a quick preview of what you'll find in each chapter:

- **Chapter 1, "Cultivating Leadership Skills in Students,"** will explore the significance of learning standards in shaping classroom dynamics, fostering student growth, and nurturing leadership qualities. It will offer insight into the seamless integration of standards with lesson design and will empower you to create classrooms that prioritize academic achievement alongside a culture of leadership and lifelong learning.

- **Chapter 2, "A Vision for Student Success,"** explores what defines student success, emphasizing the importance of authentic learning, problem-solving, and varied experiences in the learning process. It also introduces a helpful framework—AIM—that includes all aspects of a successful student. You'll learn about strategies for creating time and space for students to explore and engage in authentic learning moments, as well as have the opportunity to critically reflect on your approach to designing engaging learning. To help, the chapter offers collaborative discussion prompts to explore further and strategies for student success to implement within your personal learning network (PLN) and beyond.

- In **Chapter 3, "Every Learner Is a Leader,"** we challenge the conventional notion of leadership by emphasizing that *all* students possess leadership potential. By shifting conventional classroom dynamics, you can help students begin to believe they are leaders. By leveraging principles of Universal Design for Learning (UDL) and exploring avenues for representation, engagement, and expression, you can create environments where every student can step into leadership roles and thrive.

- **Chapter 4, "Student Entrepreneurship,"** explores the intersection of education and entrepreneurship, guiding you to support your students' recognition of their strengths, passions, and future endeavors. You will learn how to ally with all stakeholders (students, parents, community members, school leaders, and fellow educators) to expand required learning to real-world applications, thereby bridging the gap from classroom learning to future jobs and personal development. Students become more confident thinkers through activities that promote financial literacy, social networking, and project management.

- **Chapter 5, "Promoting Problem-Solving with Students,"** addresses critical problem-solving skills and their importance for success in higher education and future careers. You'll learn how to leverage problem-solving strategies and frameworks to create a classroom culture that closely aligns with real-world experiences, giving students the background knowledge and practice they need in order to comfortably transition into any role or experience they choose.

- **Chapter 6, "Innovative Thinking: The Cornerstone of Authentic Assessment,"** explores how fostering innovative thinking can revolutionize assessment practices. It challenges traditional assessment methods by highlighting the limitations of completion-only work and standardized testing before delving into the importance of creativity, idea generation, and student expression for more authentic assessment.

- **Chapter 7, "Digital Portfolios: The Future of CVs,"** looks ahead to the evolving landscape of resumes and CVs, showcasing how digital portfolios provide tangible evidence of student learning, creativity, and engagement. Any collection (big or small) of learning achievements empowers students in a powerful way to take ownership of their learning journey and showcase their unique talents and achievements in and outside the classroom.

- **Chapter 8, "Completing the Learning Cycle: Reflection and Feedback,"** addresses the challenge of setting aside time for reflection and feedback within the learning process. Feedback's significance in enhancing student learning and achievement cannot be overstated, so this chapter discusses practical strategies for modeling and teaching student reflection and feedback. In it, you'll also find resources to help you provide continuous improvement and empowerment in your classroom.

- In **Chapter 9, "Teaching Beyond Tradition,"** we challenge the conventional norms of teaching and learning that have led the way for decades. Traditionally, education has often been burdened with memorization and repetitive practice, restricting curiosity and creativity. In today's ever-evolving world, however, such methods fail to prepare students for the challenges ahead. This chapter advocates a shift toward nontraditional teaching methods, prioritizing holistic student development. You will explore innovative approaches that nurture social learning, emotional intelligence, and individualized learning experiences. By fostering environments that encourage curiosity and creativity, you can genuinely empower your students to thrive

Every learner has the potential to lead, create, and thrive. This book is a guide for educators and learners who want to go beyond the typical classroom and reimagine what it means to teach, learn, and innovate. Looking through the lens of student leadership and entrepreneurship, we will show you how to empower students to develop new skills and refine existing ones. Whether you are a seasoned educator looking for inspiration or new to the idea of merging entrepreneurship and classroom learning, we want to help you build powerful learning experiences that reignite both you and your students. Because when students succeed, we all succeed.

CHAPTER 1

Cultivating Leadership Skills in Students

Standards and Principles Addressed

The content of this chapter aligns with the following standards, indicators, and principles:

ISTE Student Standards

Empowered Learner (1.1.a, 1.1.b)

Knowledge Constructor (1.3.d)

ISTE Educator Standards

Learner (2.1.a)

Leader (2.2.a)

Collaborator (2.4.b)

Designer (2.5.b)

Facilitator (2.6.a)

Transformational Learning Principles

Nurture: Cultivate Belonging, Connect Learning to Learner

Guide: Spark Curiosity

Empower: Ignite Agency

Leadership Skills: The Essential Student Toolkit

If you were to list the top three leadership skills and then ask a group of students to do the same, the results would vary from person to person because everyone's values, personalities, and experiences with leadership are so different. It is important to consider this in a learning environment and to explore both personal and professional aspects of effective leadership before incorporating them into curriculum and learning activities.

Personal leadership skills help individuals manage their lives, relationships, and growth effectively, contributing to personal success and well-being. Professional leadership will foster a positive work culture, inspire and motivate teams, and drive innovative change (Winston & Patterson, 2006). Leadership skills—communication, critical and analytic thinking, problem-solving, ideation and innovation, conflict resolution, time and project management, and emotional intelligence—are needed to execute jobs and projects, as well as to guide and lead teams. These can be *hard skills* that pertain to job-related competencies or *soft skills*, such as personal qualities and all-encompassing characteristics that can easily be seen by others through an individual's communication, problem-solving, and guided mentorship.

So, why do leadership skills matter for students? Some would argue that leadership skills and strategies are necessary for those in management—CEOs, project managers, or the like—and involve proficiency in negotiation, communication, conflict resolution, decision-making, relationship building, and so much more (Coursera Staff, 2024). We challenge this idea that leadership skills can be developed for only those with "important titles" and *firmly* take the stance that understanding how to lead yourself and others is imperative for anyone making decisions, *including* students.

Before a student arrives in the classroom, much of the instructional day has already been planned out for them. Their schedule, study periods, where to learn, when to learn, where to sit, when to eat, when to take breaks, what and how information is communicated, how to receive it, and how to show evidence of learning are all decisions already made on behalf of the student.

We asked a small group of middle and high school students: "As a student in middle school or high school, what decisions did *you* get to make during the school day/year?" Here is a sample of their responses:

- my lunch spot
- extracurricular activity from a limited list
- to take advanced classes or regular classes
- where to park
- to participate or not
- how much effort to put into assignments
- which pencil case or folder to use

These are not the kinds of decisions that will help them thrive in their futures. If we want to give students the confidence and practice to become transformative leaders, we must give them opportunities to make impactful decisions that have significant and noticeable effects. Over time, we must pass the responsibility over to them, first for small decisions with minimal consequences and then gradually to larger, high-impact decisions. By giving students this agency, we ensure that their confidence and competence in their own abilities will increase.

According to the World Economic Forum, the top ten skills needed by 2025 for everyone, teachers and students alike, include:

- analytical thinking and innovation
- active learning and learning strategies
- complex problem-solving
- critical thinking and analysis
- creativity, originality, and initiative
- leadership and social influence
- technology use
- technology design and programming
- stress tolerance, resilience, and flexibility
- reasoning and ideation (Whiting, 2020)

In addition, over half of the workforce will need to "reskill" due to the double disruption of the 2020 pandemic and technological advancements like artificial intelligence (Whiting, 2020). To prepare them for this future, we need to place students in learning situations that require them to practice critical thinking skills and that foster other listed skills.

Cultivating Leadership Skills with Learning Standards

Learning standards are meant to be a goal-setting method for both teacher and student to gauge learning progress and evaluate the need for reteaching or supplemental support. Assessments for learning give insight into where students' learning may land at the beginning, middle, and end of a school year; however, timeframes for receiving feedback are lengthy and students have often moved on to the next grade level or even graduated by the time a teacher has the chance to assess results. Supplemental standards like the ISTE Standards for Students and Educators and the ISTE+ASCD Transformational Learning Principles (TLPs) can set up skills and knowledge for students that support meeting required learning standards but also set up students for success beyond the classroom. Standards and principles that support leadership in students are a great way to develop growth as educators, too.

Many leadership skills seem almost identical to the ISTE Student and Educator Standards as well as the TLPs. Students leading themselves to be Empowered Learners (Student Standard 1.1.a) who articulate and set goals, develop strategies, and reflect to improve also become adults who find comfort in decision-making and communicating by both speaking and listening well. They learn to cultivate belonging and celebrate others (TLP Nurture). Students who become Innovative Designers (Student Standards 1.4.a, 1.4.c, 1.4.d) who know and use the design process, generate ideas, and solve authentic problems also become adults who are analytical thinkers, creative designers, and project managers. They go out looking for authentic experiences, lead themselves to be curious, and skillfully refine their expertise (TLPs Guide, Empower). When we teach our students about leadership, we are also teaching ourselves to master the same skills. Doing this over and over each day creates a continuous loop of learning, reflection, and risk-taking that eventually empowers both the teacher and the learner to level up their learning and real-world experiences.

Connecting Curriculum and Student Empowerment

What if you asked a group of fourth-grade students, "How can we create a game that teaches people about body systems?" Imagine having them sort through curriculum statements to identify the driving learning standards and supporting standards, and then making prior learning connections from math, science, writing, and design classes.

If this scenario sounds too good to be true, Kris Leverton, an instructional coach and curriculum leader in the UK, would beg to differ. He witnessed this powerful and successful learning scenario firsthand. Working in groups, students took advantage of this empowering opportunity, building on their expertise and challenging themselves at the same time. As Leverton (2021) explained, "Students clearly chose supporting standards that emphasized their own strengths (such as drawing skills) but also had the chance to focus on areas of the curriculum that they felt they needed to practice." He concluded:

> Creating a culture of shared responsibility and ownership of the curriculum can be an important part of developing student agency. This approach is not limited to group-based project-based learning (PBL) units; it can also be valuable when setting personal learning goals or working on individual projects. (Leverton, 2021)

When students are allowed to lead, they show up and often surpass expectations. Because students have been immersed in environments rooted in the Prussian Model of a classroom (age-based with desks in rows and columns all pointing to the teacher) and often not given room to test their leadership capabilities, the natural assumption is that students cannot lead themselves or others. Our stance is that students *can* lead, and this book will urge you to rethink your learning environment, your approach to student leadership, and how the same standards required by others can be an opportunity to flip the script on classrooms of the past and begin cultivating leaders now.

A supportive learning environment that fosters student leadership gives learners security and confidence (Grigoropoulos, 2021). They become more comfortable with risk-taking, individuality, identifying strengths and weaknesses, and collaborative learning and feedback. Several things happen simultaneously when students are immersed in this classroom or school culture. Social and emotional support through collaborative learning teaches emotional intelligence, and individualized and project-based learning teaches self-assessment and self-advocacy. Through choice-based activities and projects, students learn to lead on the accommodations they need to fit their different learning paces and abilities. Opportunities for performance-based or authentic learning teach the process of giving and receiving helpful feedback from teachers and peers and the chance to refine the self-reflection process. Giving students exposure to varied assessments, especially performance-based and authentic assessments, teaches students that they are not just defined by a single score or grade, but that they have value, skills, and talents that are needed for real-world application.

Pairing learning standards with leadership skills is a superpower for students and teachers. It firmly helps students connect to how the present learning in their classroom will boost their knowledge and set them apart as they move forward into college and career paths. To create a supportive learning environment that fosters student leadership while meeting expectations to teach learning standards, start with the required learning standards (Common Core, TEKS, Standards of Learning Framework, and similar). These standards are the focus when looking at the curriculum year-at-a-glance in detail and are used to drive all projects, activities, and assessments. Typically, these standards will be non-negotiable.

Next, determine which supplemental standards or learning principles (ISTE Standards, TLPs, the Future Ready Framework, and the like) best support the required standards. There are many options, but it is best to look for principles that align with the teaching philosophy of all learning stakeholders.

Last, have students engage and reflect on their leadership skills for today and tomorrow. Find out what they believe is important for their future and fuse them with the required standards and chosen principles. This might be an opportunity to utilize a collaborative activity, gather video feedback from individual students, accept student-designed infographics, or simply use the commenting features of a learning management system. The goal is to give students the opportunity for ownership. They do not necessarily have a voice when required standards are implemented and might not be aware supplemental principles exist. Still, leadership skills are something they have most likely picked up, no matter their age or learning ability. When students can give voice to the leadership skills that they believe are most beneficial, they possess a sense of ownership over the process and implementation.

The exchange of ownership is the dynamic moment when students, not just teachers, have a vested interest in their learning outcomes. Empowering students to take charge of their learning makes them more likely to dive deeper into their interests, which leads them to set forth goals toward future careers and accomplishments thoughtfully. Additionally, student autonomy creates checks and balances, and students begin to hold themselves and each other accountable.

Implementation can begin once everyone fully understands the required learning standards, supplemental standards, and targeted leadership skills. Implementing these skills within your teaching practice is probably not a new idea, as you most likely already use many of these strategies daily.

- **Teach:** Review classroom, school, or district leader qualities and provide examples and activities that promote thoughtful understanding of each leadership quality.

- **Model:** Educators naturally serve as role models by demonstrating behaviors in their interactions with students and colleagues. Modeling leadership with day-to-day interactions will inspire students to mirror and develop their own leadership behaviors and habits.

- **Create Opportunity:** During lesson design, spot and incorporate opportunities for students to take on leadership roles within the classroom, during group projects, or school community events. Practicing confident decision-making supports the skills needed for advancement and future endeavors.

- **Empower:** Empower students to embrace challenges and practice open-mindedness with new ideas, strategies, and activities. Build time into each unit and lesson to allow for intentional self-reflection, journaling, discussion, and/or student-led conferences to promote increased self-awareness.

- **Thought Partner:** Find other educators, administrators, or coaches who value the development and implementation of leadership skills with learning standards so that there is an ongoing exchange of what works, what needs to be refined, and how to continue to innovate and create change for student learning.

Challenges and Opportunities

Ideas and innovation are exciting until it is time to sit down and begin planning and executing the steps involved with a new idea. The planning stage reveals challenges not always thought out in the initial ideation, and executing a new idea can seem overwhelming with any new strategy or implementation. Challenges in the classroom will always be an obstacle, as Rose (2012) explained:

> Today, our collective vision for education is broader, our nation is more complex and diverse, and our technical capabilities are more powerful. But we continue to assume the factory-model classroom and its rigid bell schedules, credit requirements, age-based grade levels, and physical specifications when we talk about school reform.
>
> That's why the promise of educational innovation is less about processing power and software code and more about the opportunity to release ourselves from general assumptions regarding how instruction is organized and delivered.

According to an ASCD survey with hundreds of responses, there are currently ten main obstacles educators face today: teacher retention, student behavior, outdated learning models, understanding and implementing equity, student engagement, teacher workload, learning gaps, mental health, respect for educators, and curriculum criticism (McKibben, 2023). Struggles in K–12 education often seem overwhelming, systemic, and rooted against all signs of innovation and change.

If you are an educator or administrator reading this right now, you were most likely inspired by an educator in your own life or sought the profession to make a difference in youth and future leaders. Many of you have overcome huge obstacles personally and professionally to be where you are now. It is that thread of inspiration and hope we ask you to find as you continue through each chapter, each idea, and each challenge. As a whole, educators have always turned obstacles and adversities into advantages. Often, however, we each get so focused on the problem of what is not going right that we do not allow room for a solution. There are concrete solutions teachers can adopt individually, and school leaders can ensure organizationally, that can have a major impact on the success and well-being of educators and the students they serve (Mielke, 2023).

For example, the demands on teachers' time often limits their ability to give meaningful feedback on activities or projects when it is needed most. One solution is to shift part of that responsibility to students. At the beginning of each unit or lesson, incorporate time to teach students appropriate feedback guidelines with specific examples and modeling. Students improve their performance as they experience more specific, immediate feedback (Mielke, 2023). It takes a mindset shift to remember that teachers do not spend all their time teaching students. The majority of time is taken for administrative tasks, meetings, lesson planning, grading, professional development, and extra duties. There is power in recognizing limitations and knowing that not all things will get done perfectly, but rather understanding that prioritizing a few things and doing them exceptionally well will yield success for you and your students.

Bringing Standards and Leadership Together

The power of student leadership skills is exponential. Learning standards are a great way to keep learning focused and moving in the right direction, and pairing the standards with leadership strategies only reinforces to the students that the experiences they have in a classroom also support the skills necessary for them to be the most confident and empowered out in the real world. Implementation of this pairing is a steady process, but once it's understood, developed, and refined, the outcome is worth the investment of time and effort: Students' abilities will evolve so powerfully that they likely will outperform your expectations, setting them up to overachieve personally and professionally.

But a few questions remain:

- How can you implement student leadership strategies alongside learning standards while meeting expectations for high-stakes testing?
- How can you design activities and projects that empower student leadership and save teachers time?
- How can you scale authentic experiences for students and create space for students to perform skills that showcase their learning?

This book's goal is to help you answer these questions and give you the confidence and inspiration to begin leading your students to lead themselves, changing the course of leadership and education altogether. The following chapters will take you on a journey that enhances your skill set. They will enable you to guide the growth and learning of the next generation, paving the way for them into the real world. Through problem-solving, entrepreneurship, creativity, and more, together we all will celebrate the power of student-led learning in and out of the classroom. Students *can* lead. Students *want* to lead. We just need to create experiences that allow them to do so.

**tinyurl.com/
TodaysLearners**

Scan the QR code to access resources associated with this chapter.

CHAPTER 2

A Vision for Student Success

Standards and Principles Addressed

The content of this chapter aligns with the following standards, indicators, and principles:

ISTE Student Standards

Empowered Learner (1.1.a, 1.1.b)

ISTE Educator Standards

Learner (2.1.a, 2.1.c)

Leader (2.2.a, 2.2.b)

Facilitator (2.6.a, 2.6.c, 2.6.d)

Transformational Learning Principles

Empower: Prioritize Authentic Experiences, Ignite Agency

Defining Student Success

Standards and curriculum provide yardsticks to measure student progress. They're relatively uniform nationwide or statewide with slight variations, but they don't tell the whole story of student success. Ask any group of educators how they describe student success, and you'll hear multiple definitions and opinions. The typical expectation of student success comes not just from the nation or the state but also from the communities, the school boards, the educators, and the parents. Everyone looks at student success through their unique lens and perspective.

Yes, success can be whatever we say it is, but too many factors and opinions can impact student success adversely. Each group of stakeholders may aim for a variety of outcomes using entirely different measures. Suppose the stakeholders cannot come to a unified agreement on what success is. In this case, everyone will continue going in different directions and never reach the end goal: empowered students who are confident to begin college and a career.

For example, state laws impact some variables; other variables may include academic achievement expectations, teacher availability, and available resources to support student achievement initiatives. Critical thinking, problem-solving, and student well-being may be overlooked if a school is focused solely on grades for status. Stakeholders lead the vision for student success, but if they cannot get clear on the vision, they will not be able to communicate and execute it for students.

Many Perspectives, Varied Success

So, what *does* it mean to be a successful student? What does it mean to be a successful graduate? How can curriculum-based learning be combined with more fluid experiences for learners who become leaders? Consider the perspectives of a recent graduate and a student.

Avery Davenport, a twenty-year-old high school graduate and small business manager, said:

> Every student is different. They come from different backgrounds, upbringings, experiences, and cultures. Success can vary. Success looked different for me when I was an eighteen-year-old twelfth grader compared to when I was three, and it is drastically evolving even now. The weight of a letter or a number does not matter as much as my opinion of my own work and progress. **—AVERY**

Eighth grader Douglas Palmer, who is taking classes to increase his leadership skills, shared his thoughts with educators during a live public webinar:

> Student success, to me, is about excelling academically, demonstrating outstanding leadership skills, and eventually securing a career that brings happiness. It involves achieving excellent grades, being a supportive, effective leader, and ultimately being a well-rounded student. **—DOUGLAS**

Meanwhile, most states classify success as completing the correct number of courses, demonstrating a high grade-point average (GPA), and being admitted to a college or getting a head start in a career (Stanford, 2023). This definition of success has become ingrained in our students as the only marker of achievement, and often, students feel that if they are not receiving affirmation in the form of academic awards, they are not successful. Awards and recognition by mass audiences are incredibly validating, but showing up consistently and contributing their best in the circles they belong to are also a win. A single grade or an award wholly defines none of us. Fortunately, at least seventeen states have exceeded traditional expectations by creating a guiding document outlining goals that influence education policy (Stanford, 2023). They are usually titled "Portrait of a Graduate," "Profile of a Graduate," or similar.

Some districts have these portraits or profiles, while others list future-ready characteristics or skill sets for students to achieve. During our research for this book, we found many varied lists of skills and competencies to ensure students' preparedness for life after high school. Combing through them rapidly became tedious and frustrating because no two lists were identical. Many lists had similar skills, characteristics, and a vision for what graduates would be as they enter college or a career. Still, much like the learning standards in the 1800s, these lists offered many different thoughts on what the end goal for high school graduates should be.

The AIM Framework

So, what are the commonalities of all these perspectives on student success? We knew we needed to identify them because these commonalities become key attributes and characteristics in which students can strive to excel. To better understand the bigger picture, we looked at graduate profiles, future-ready characteristics, and lists of future skills necessary for all students and professionals. Then, we focused on the post–high school students and their next steps in life: college or the start of a career. In this instance, the college and the employer are the primary stakeholders for student success, and both groups may be looking more holistically at success and its benchmarks. We found the commonalities within each list and then developed a guide, or framework, to help schools and parents bridge students' success from middle school to high school to college and career. We called this framework AIM, which stands for **A**cademic Excellence, Interpersonal Skills, and **M**astery of Self.

Our findings showed that stakeholders consistently focus on three specific areas of skills and characteristics to aid students in transitioning from school to college or career. To mold each student into a confident, successful contributor to society, school leaders and educators should build all three areas of the framework into their curriculum (FIGURE 2.1). These are the foundational skills with which students need guidance and mentorship along their learning journey. When you combine AIM with state standards, district technology policies, graduate profiles, and external organization principles (ISTE Standards, Transformational Learning Principles (TLPs), TCEA Essential Learning Expectations, and similar) you will level up the success of the whole student.

FIGURE 2.1
Student success is built on the adoption of each piece of AIM.

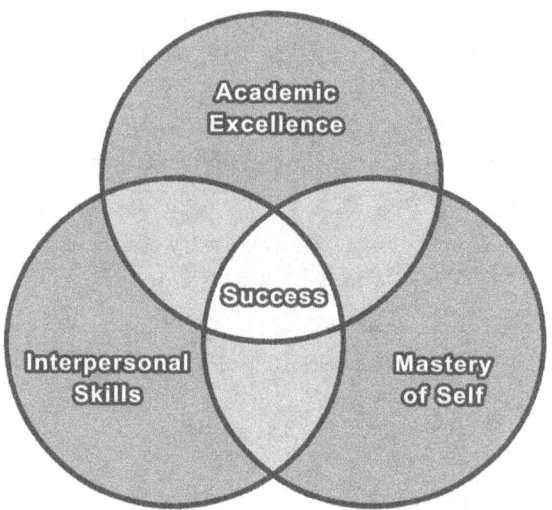

Take a closer look at the skills in each area of AIM (FIGURE 2.2).

Academic excellence	Interpersonal skills	Mastery of self
Application of knowledge	Leadership (trustworthiness, respectfulness, integrity)	Self-reliance
Critical, innovative thinking	Social influence	Sense of belonging
Problem-solving	Effective communication	Reflectiveness and self-awareness
Creativity and creative expression	Networking ability	Resiliency and persistence
Engaged, empowered learning	Collaboration skills	Confidence
Global collaboration and awareness	Empathy and kindness	Self-discipline
Information analysis and evaluation	Service orientation	Decision-making
Self-directed learning	Perspective inclusivity	Open-mindedness and curiosity
		Goal setting

FIGURE 2.2
The AIM Framework

AIM considers every stakeholder's desire for success while supporting all students at any point in their learning journey and future careers. *Academic Excellence* primarily focuses on learning and cognitive abilities. *Interpersonal Skills* support students as they learn to interact with others, and *Mastery of Self* is a set of core character skills needed for continuous growth. Each of these areas will challenge the student in such a way they will be more prepared for higher education or work environments. The AIM Framework was intentionally integrated as the overall theme of each of the following chapters and is at the heart of every strategy and perspective presented.

Authentic Learning for Student Success

Authentic learning illustrates a specific skill or behavior in a real-life context. As mentioned in Chapter 1, authentic learning (or assessments) is not the same as performance-based learning (or assessments). Authentic learning is critical for student success because it is the variable that launches students to success beyond high school. Authentic learning provides organic problem-solving experiences for the student and forges a path to a well-rounded learner and leader. Academic Excellence works as a stand-alone goal, but if you want to supercharge authentic learning, pair it with Interpersonal Skills and/or Mastery of Self skills. This practice helps to motivate students by answering their why before they ask for one and encourages them to understand how the learning now directly relates to meeting their future goals.

Authentic learning and assessment are based on the Constructivist Theory, which underlies how students construct new meaning and knowledge (Messier 2022). This theory states that instruction is a hands-on approach, and instructors are facilitators of knowledge instead of the holders of all knowledge (Ertmer & Newby, 1993). Practice of this theory includes minimal teacher guidance, an abundance of classroom resources, and minimal memorization (Davis, 2009). This theory emphasizes skills rather than content and allows students to focus on discovering solutions rather than being shown solutions already discovered by others (Davis, 2009).

Authentic learning can take many forms, such as:

- student-created podcasts
- production of videos
- portfolios or showcases
- composing a song
- internships
- service-learning projects
- simulations
- audio/video interviews
- collaboration projects with businesses
- inquiry-based lessons

In early 2024, the US Department of Education released a National Education Technology Plan (FIGURE 2.3). The plan is a call to action for closing divides in three main areas: digital access, digital design, and digital use (Klein, 2024).

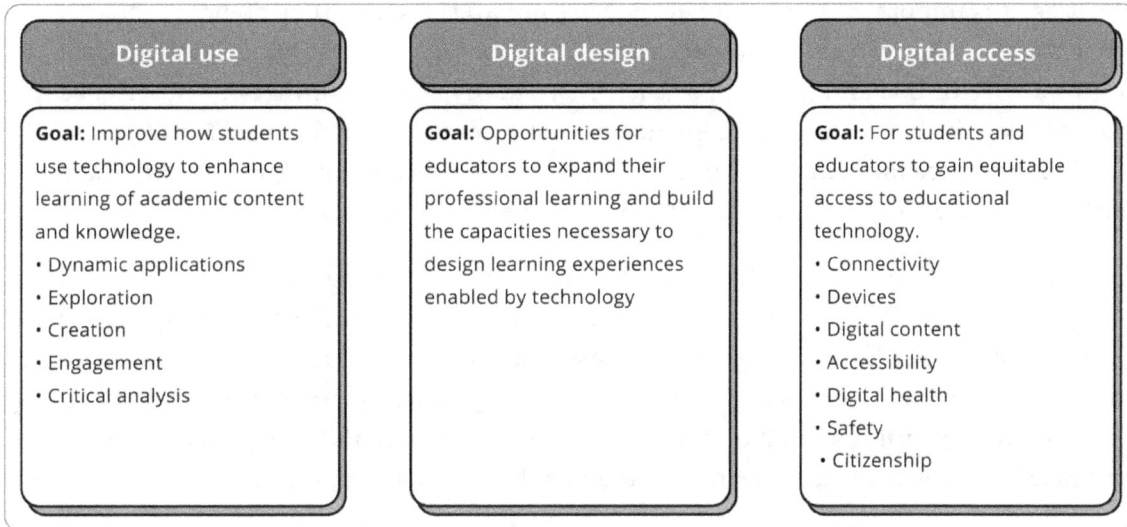

Digital use	Digital design	Digital access
Goal: Improve how students use technology to enhance learning of academic content and knowledge. • Dynamic applications • Exploration • Creation • Engagement • Critical analysis	**Goal:** Opportunities for educators to expand their professional learning and build the capacities necessary to design learning experiences enabled by technology	**Goal:** For students and educators to gain equitable access to educational technology. • Connectivity • Devices • Digital content • Accessibility • Digital health • Safety • Citizenship

FIGURE 2.3
The National Education Technology Plan 2024

The plan points out that instead of students using technology devices simply to watch videos or check email, educators should strive to model and use technology to code, collaborate, or create (digital use). To make this a reality, students need devices, connectivity, accessibility to digital content, and opportunities to practice digital citizenship, digital safety, and digital health (digital access). Empowered teachers who design learning experiences with the goal of authentic learning (FIGURE 2.4) in mind create empowered students who can confidently choose the medium in which they express their learning thoughtfully and reflect on where they have been, where they are now, and which direction their learning should take (digital design). This plan supports the AIM Framework by reiterating the idea that designing learning experiences that surpass baseline requirements molds students into creators rather than only consumers of digital content.

For example, creating choice boards with authentic projects, checkpoints, and activities that align with learning standards gives students autonomy to practice decision-making (Mastery of Self, AIM) on how best to present what they know. It also gives the experience of setting small achievable goals to complete larger tasks and creates moments of built-in reflection for students to ask questions and clarify misconceptions (Mastery of Self, AIM). Students need more time to think and process to best connect the knowledge to the activity and the result (Academic Excellence, AIM). As we work with students of all abilities, it is important to remember they are not all the same; they do not receive information in the same way, they do not process information at the same speed, and their brains are as unique and set apart as their DNA. Many need an immersive experience for learning to stick! Additionally, to ensure students are prepared for their future, classroom experiences must include opportunities for collaboration with peers and practice with active listening and communication (Interpersonal Skills, AIM).

Utilizing the technology available to teach digital citizenship, media literacy, and effective use of technology while using the AIM Framework, learning standards, and supplemental principles only solidifies the projected success of a student. Equipping each student with as many opportunities to problem-solve, think critically, and implement the design thinking process not only builds a solid foundation for their future but also sets each on a course to embrace how they think and learn and adapt as they grow and mature.

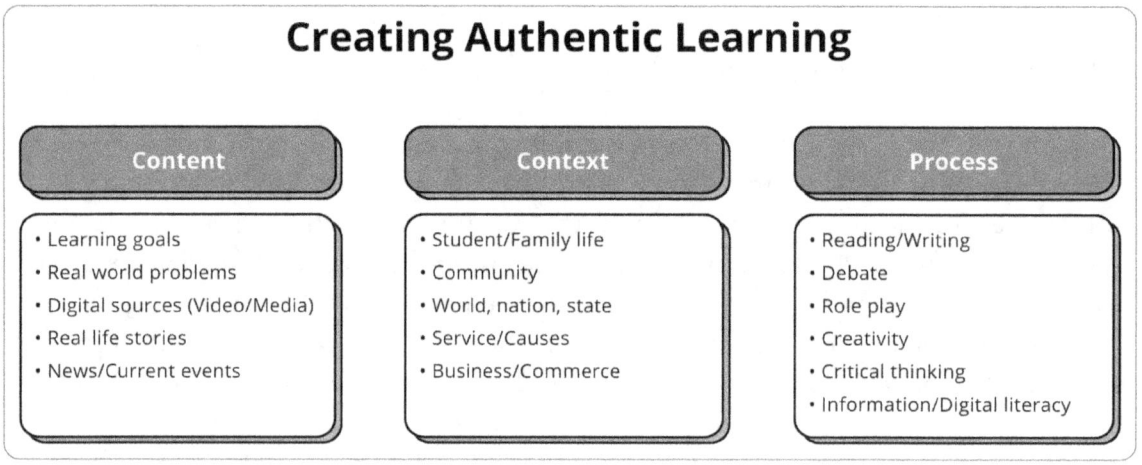

FIGURE 2.4
The three steps of authentic learning

Aligning and Iterating with Standards

Our current system works and focuses heavily on the academic aspect of student success, with Common Core Standards and state curriculum taking the driver's seat. Changing the idea of success, especially as it has been ingrained into the education system for decades, is no small feat—but it is possible. Even though many aspects of traditional learning environments are out of the control of both student and teacher, there are feasible strategies that you can incorporate into your daily work to refine a process that truly serves students. When molding glass, the molten glass can be shaped and bent into the desired form once the temperature reaches the required value. In the same way, educators can mold dynamic learning activities into experiences that far exceed the original intent of the learning standards.

When creating authentic learning experiences for students, always first begin with your required standards and learning objectives, pairing several standards together for a single lesson or project. For example, a science teacher might combine engineering practices where a student should ask questions, identify problems, and share investigative findings (Texas Education Agency, 2021) and evaluate evidence and credibility from different sources (information literacy). This would meet the academic aspect of learning. Still, to deepen the understanding and incorporate AIM or additional principles (ISTE Standards, TLPs), the lesson might require students to work together collaborating on a single document, reviewing the work of all contributors (collaboration and communication), and then work on individual parts to bring to life a whole product as listed above (authentic learning). Bringing together all parts into a whole learning experience allows students to reach self-mastery by completing the learning process from new knowledge to application and spending more time and space thinking through their curiosity, questions, misconceptions, and reflections.

Aligning state standards with the AIM Framework, ISTE Standards, and TLPs will become crucial for preparing well-rounded students with the necessary skills to succeed in real-world environments. Educators can create a supportive and challenging environment that fosters holistic development and lifelong success by focusing on Academic Excellence, Interpersonal Skills, and Mastery of Self. By providing the right environment, facilitating, and giving students room to explore, we can help students meet and surpass the typical learning objectives (McGathey, 2018).

Reflection Strategies and Success

Throughout this book, you will hear how important student reflection is to drive student success and will learn strategies to implement it in the learning process. Making time for educators to reflect on their instruction can affect the success of their students just as directly. As busy educators work from sunup to sundown meeting the expectations set forth upon them, it is easy to lose sight of how to firmly complete the learning cycle:

reflection. Instructional strategies that create time and space for students to explore and engage in authentic learning experiences are ever-changing and transforming. What works for one educator and class might not be the best approach for another. What works with one class of students one year might not be a right fit for the next group. Additionally, learning how to balance challenging experiences alongside required standards is at times difficult but not impossible. The success of this directly correlates to the mindset of the educational stakeholders with teachers leading. It is important to remember that as teachers we will not get it right one hundred percent of the time. We would never ask our students to simply give up if they do not get it right the first time—we shouldn't do so either. The only way to test if an idea will work is to try and then be ready to modify it.

Reflection is at the core of Kolb's Experiential Learning concept, as well. Essentially this approach is made up of three key shifts in the student-teacher dynamic: The teacher becomes more of a facilitator guiding students, students solve real-world problems or simulations, and students participate in reflections of their experience. This last is key: Students need to think about how they have solved problems and draw conclusions (Kharbach, 2024). The most important part of this concept is reflection because students are not just *doing,* they are *thinking,* and because this is the most critical portion of the learning cycle, it is also the main ingredient for success—not just for students but also for teachers. It is imperative that we analyze our experiences, understand the purpose of certain actions or behaviors, and draw conclusions on the result of changes in our process.

It is important for as an educator to, first, lean heavily on your content expertise and the tried-and-true instructional strategies that work for you. Next, you must look at your lesson design and ask yourself:

- What is outdated?
- What can be modified?
- How is technology incorporated and integrated into the activities?
- Am I nudging my students to rely less on me to have all the answers?
- Who is doing most of the speaking during a lesson or activity?
- Who is making the most decisions during the application and practice of skills?
- What is the process for student reflection?
- How are students receiving and giving feedback?

To be able to transform our classrooms into spaces that allow for more exploration, innovation, and collaboration, we cannot continue to avoid reflecting on our own instructional practices and mindsets. By devoting time to our own reflection, we are better able to allow our students time for the same reflective practice.

Transforming Student Success

Take a closer look at AIM and each stakeholder's focal points of success. The educator is the only stakeholder that is truly aiming to achieve *all* the skills and characteristics listed in the framework. Educators know that academic excellence is vital, but they also see how interpersonal skills and self-mastery places each student on a path that leads to continued success past high school graduation.

To prepare for the following chapters, think through some driving questions to help you begin discussions with your administrative team and colleagues on how best to merge a different measure of success into your school. To help you and your colleagues, here are a few questions, prompts, and ideas for transforming the picture of a successful student:

- How do we define student success and measure it beyond academic achievement?

- How do we reach personal and interpersonal success for each learner?

- What experiences do we need to create for students to feel confident and comfortably thrive in college and the real world?

- How do we balance academic achievement and emotional intelligence?

- How can we incorporate adaptability and resilience into classrooms?

- What scenarios can we create that offer collaboration and communication to create shifts in student-teacher mindsets?

- How can we integrate key stakeholders to support evolving curriculum, portrait of graduate characteristics, and ongoing change?

- How can we ensure our practices and policies equip learning as a lifelong journey for our students?

What's Next?

Success should never be defined by anyone but us, with each of us embracing all that we are. Yet, students wake up every day and are led to believe if they are not successful in the eyes of academia or a standardized test, they will not be able to "make it" in the world. The irony of this becomes clear when students grow out of a classroom learning environment into the real world because it is there that they are truly tested with what they know and how they can apply their knowledge.

In their books, James Carse and Simon Sinek both write about finite and infinite games. Typical success for students in school is finite, as it has fixed rules, clear objectives, and defined endpoints (Fitzpatrick, 2024). The action item we are proposing in this chapter and throughout the book is to create a learning environment that is more infinite: ongoing, evolving, and continuous. When we can show students their value and ideas are also important to their overall success, we can finally begin shifting learning environments and seeing different results in our students and, in turn, create confident and transformative leaders.

tinyurl.com/ TodaysLearners

Scan the QR code to access resources associated with this chapter.

CHAPTER 3

Every Learner Is a Leader

Standards and Principles Addressed

The content of this chapter aligns with the following standards, indicators, and principles:

ISTE Student Standards

Empowered Learner (1.1.a, 1.1.b, 1.1.c)

Knowledge Constructor (1.3.a, 1.3.d)

Innovative Designer (1.4.a, 1.4.b, 1.4.c, 1.4.d)

Global Collaborator (1.7.a, 1.7.b, 1.7.c, 1.7.d)

ISTE Educator Standards

Learner (2.1.a, 2.1.b, 2.1.c)

Leader (2.2.a, 2.2.b, 2.2.c)

Designer (2.5.b, 2.5.c)

Transformational Learning Principles

Nurture: Connect Learning to Learner, Ensure Equity

Guide: Spark Curiosity, Develop Expertise, Elevate Reflection

Empower: Prioritize Authentic Experiences, Ignite Agency

Inclusive Leadership

In many classrooms, the conventional notion of leadership is often associated with high-performing students or those who consistently achieve top grades and outperform traditional academic tasks. Although this view aligns with student success in schools that focus on grades and high graduation completion, it limits the understanding of leadership and excludes most students from opportunities to develop and demonstrate leadership skills early on.

The focus needs to shift from academic performance to a broader range of traits and abilities to integrate the idea that every learner has leadership potential regardless of age or background. Leadership involves visionary thinking, effective communication, integrity, empathy, adaptability, and the ability to collaborate and resolve conflicts—qualities not exclusive to academic assessments or tasks. By identifying, encouraging, and strengthening these traits in all students, educators can foster an environment and culture where every learner can step into a leadership role.

For example, Juli Parsons is a twenty-three-year-old college graduate with not one but two business degrees, who is now pursuing additional skills in programming and data analytics. Juli has experience with various learning environments and has had multiple opportunities to refine her leadership knowledge and application. She said,

> As I have grown older, adult attention deficit hyperactivity disorder [ADHD] is more apparent, though I am learning to mitigate the symptoms and find strategies that support me as I learn and now work. I must continually assess what I need to complete work or learn and often find ways to optimize my environments for productivity.
> —JULI

Every learner is unique and may display various learning challenges. Because of this, some leadership aspects could initially be difficult to instill or implement. However, when challenges and strengths are highlighted and clearly understood by the student and teacher, they become the superpowers driving students into leadership roles. The students who may struggle in a typical classroom environment, seemingly behind high-achieving students, often possess unique perspectives and problem-solving abilities that can enrich and leverage the projects and people around them. As an example, Avery Davenport gave a unique insight into the differences between students in a typical brick-and-mortar learning environment and those in untraditional spaces.

> Those who do not "fit in" or are unique make the best leaders. The ones who do not fit a mold can typically think for themselves and have a unique perspective compared to those surrounded by like-minded groups. **—AVERY**

Some students excel in critical thinking, assessment interpretation, and problem-solving; others may need more thinking time and processing before they feel they excel in a particular skill or subject, a regular occurrence during Tisha and Rick's educational journeys. Therefore, by embracing the diversity of learners and understanding each student's strengths, educators can create an inclusive environment where everyone feels heard, valued, and empowered.

Catering for such an environment requires an intentional and inclusive approach to teaching and learning. The implementation of such frameworks as Universal Design for Learning (UDL)—which we'll dive deeper into shortly—AIM, ISTE Standards, and Transformational Learning Principles (TPLs) can help you design authentic opportunities, activities, and assessments that will allow students to showcase their strengths, take on leadership roles, and contribute to the classroom in meaningful ways.

By introducing and transforming leadership skills in the classroom and embracing the diversity of students' abilities, together we can develop a generation of academically proficient leaders who are also empathetic, resilient, and collaborative. This inclusive approach will benefit all students, enabling them to realize their full potential and contribute positively and impactfully to their communities.

Task-Orientated and Relationship-Orientated Leadership

Task-oriented and relationship-oriented leadership focus on two different aspects of leading and guiding. *Task-oriented leadership* focuses on a structured environment with direct communication to ensure tasks are completed and goals are reached. Task-oriented leadership might also be described as *transactional leadership*, whereas leaders interact with their followers only in limited verbal interactions revolving around performance (Aarons, 2006). *Relationship-oriented leadership* is focused on supportive and participative environments with peers, using empathetic communication to ensure cooperation and satisfaction within the group.

> The best leaders possess the maturity to know what and when things matter and when they do not. Some leaders have reactive responses that worsen the issue or raise group tensions, and some leaders know a simple, proactive approach can be enough.
>
> **—JULI**

Relationship-oriented leaders are often described as transformational leaders who create a vision, inspire, and build a culture of trust, innovation, and openness (Aarons, 2006). Both styles have their strengths and can be effective in different situations. Effective leaders often blend both styles, adapting their approach based on the needs of the task and the team, as Table 3.1 illustrates (Todăriţă, 2021).

TABLE 3.1 Key Differences Between Task-Oriented and Relationship-Oriented Leadership

	TASK-ORIENTED	RELATIONSHIP-ORIENTED
APPROACH	Leaders define roles, establish clear objectives, set deadlines, and develop structured plans	Leaders prioritize team morale, collaboration, and support
COMMUNICATION	Typically clear, concise, and direct	More open, empathetic, and inclusive
MOTIVATION	Driven by task achievements, rewards, and recognition based on performance	Driven by a sense of belonging, mutual respect, and personal growth
DECISION-MAKING	Made based on what is most efficient to complete a task	Made with input from the group, considering the impact on group dynamics and individual needs
CONFLICT MANAGEMENT	Managed by focusing on rules, procedures, and policies	Managed by addressing interpersonal issues and promoting understanding and cooperation

Embracing Student Leadership

Incorporating student leadership into the classroom is not just an educational strategy to enhance the learning environment but also an approach that benefits both students and educators. As a collective, we educators love to share the sentiment, "We are preparing students for their future, not ours." If we cannot point to specific instances in our classrooms where this is truly happening, however, we are missing the mark. Remember, educators best support students by guiding and facilitating their learning instead of dictating and controlling it. This approach is exemplified by Avery's story, highlighting how fostering independence and leadership transformed her educational experience and elevating her Interpersonal Skills and Mastery of Self.

> I attended a public, virtual school during the last two years of high school. This put me in charge of my time management; in some ways, I was my own teacher. There were professors, but I was responsible for ensuring assignments were turned in. I had to adapt to a new learning environment and improve my problem-solving skills. I became more independent, and in turn, my needs were met. Peers and co-workers my age who went to a traditional brick-and-mortar school did not learn these skills until after high school graduation. **—AVERY**

Five key benefits of embracing student leadership in the classroom are (King, 2023):

- ownership of learning
- peer support and mentoring
- resilience and adaptability
- positive school culture
- teacher interactions

Let's dig deeper into each.

Ownership of Learning

Studies have proven that students who are given task-orientated leadership opportunities in the classroom are more likely to take ownership of their own learning (Strong, Wynn, Irby, & Lindner, 2013). Allowing students the autonomy to make choices in their learning, actively participate in their education, set personal learning goals, and seek and evaluate resources proactively helps students develop a deeper understanding of why they are learning specific subjects at specific times and how projects and activities connect them to the skills they need for their future endeavors. As a "cherry on top," it guides students in developing a lifelong love for learning.

Peer Support and Mentoring

Peer-to-peer feedback and interactions have not always been the focus of traditional classrooms. More than likely, you and most adults have memories of learning and assessments as a siloed activity that included the student and teacher only. Over time, with the introduction of learning technologies, digital learning tools, and new instructional strategies, peer feedback and student collaboration have proven to assist the teacher with scaling and accommodating individualized learning for all. These interactions between peers help support a positive and inclusive classroom culture where students transform into leaders by practicing mentoring skills, encouragement and empathy, and a strong sense of communication. Douglas Palmer has felt these benefits.

> I find inspiration for improving my leadership skills in the older, more mature peers surrounding me. They lead by example and model how best to lead.   **—DOUGLAS**

Peer interactions need not be overplanned or overthought. Just as many companies incorporate the Yes, And . . . , method into their company culture and norms, teachers and students can agree on one approach and incorporate that into their classroom culture (Cody, 2023). There are multiple instructional strategies to incorporate this, but a few easy ideas to quickly implement now are:

- **DAB:** Deliver one compliment, ask a question, and be positive with one suggestion.
- **2 Stars, 1 Wish:** Pick two things done well and one improvement to try.
- **Prompts:** I was surprised by . . . , I am curious about . . . , I am wondering . . . , I noticed that . . .

Resilience and Adaptability

The World Economic Forum (Whiting, 2020) identified self-management skills such as resilience, stress tolerance, and flexibility as part of the top ten skills people (students and teachers alike) require in a rapidly evolving world, highlighting the importance for

Mastery of Self in relation to success. As the world changes, stressors increase, and technology transforms, there is more and more discussion about how important this topic of adaptability is for all. Leaders often face challenges and setbacks, and students are not immune to the reality of failing. However, with support and guidance from school leaders and educators, these experiences encourage students to learn to navigate stressful situations, build resilience, and adapt their actions and behaviors to a "fail forward" mentality. Juli did not always have the benefit of such teachers but found her best learning style nonetheless.

> I have been learning adaptability in my leadership and learning skills and discovered I do best in a hands-on learning environment. Doing things myself with minimal guidance and room to fail until I get it right is best for me. I have had many teachers and leaders who did not operate that way and expected me to follow the same approach. I seriously struggled when information was given only in written or verbal form.
>
> **—JULI**

With the post-pandemic change in the educational landscape, students are rebuilding their confidence and adapting to new norms as they move from students to professionals. When students learn the skill of resiliency, they are better equipped to handle change and can bring stronger critical thinking and problem-solving skills to bear.

Positive School Culture

When students are entrusted to lead in the classroom or do special school projects, it positively affects school culture. Empowered students are more likely to have increased confidence to engage in school activities, participate in decision-making processes, and contribute to their community. As mentioned, student autonomy will "flip the script" on the traditional teaching model and have students, teachers, and the entire school community changing how they approach learning, leading, and facilitating. Adopting student leadership at all levels can contribute to a positive and collaborative school culture. This inclusive environment enhances the school experience and nurtures a sense of belonging.

Teacher Interactions

When we imagine teachers, we often place them at the front of the room, controlling the information flow and dictating tasks, timing, and how information was received. No matter how knowledgeable and talented, it is a lot of responsibility for a single individual with at least thirty students to guide and teach at once. Additionally, these earlier teacher expectations did not allow students or educators to grow to their full potential. Incorporating leadership in the classroom allows you to distribute responsibilities by involving students in managing classroom activities. For example, giving students small, achievable leadership roles, such as line leader, note-taker, attendance reviewer, project lead, or tech assistant, enables you to guide students in those roles and to become a leader rather than a manager. Additionally, you can learn alongside your students and become a true learning facilitator. This collaborative approach can reduce your workload and provide you with valuable insights into students' strengths and areas for growth. In addition, teachers who support student leadership often find their classrooms more dynamic, engaged, and beneficial to the learner.

Inclusive Leadership and Learning

Inclusivity and equity are crucial in fostering a learning environment where all students receive the same opportunities and develop skills for success. Implementing the Universal Design for Learning (UDL) Guidelines, which emphasize accessibility, inclusivity, student engagement, support for diverse learning, and enhancing student learning outcomes, can support an environment that strives to help all students become leaders (Meyer et al., 2014). When incorporating leadership into learning, we must ask ourselves, "Is there another way?"

At one time, Tisha focused on state standards for Principles of Information Technology when working with students in the classroom. Yet, she redesigned the learning experience following UDL Guidelines. (You can review these guidelines by scanning the QR code at the end of this chapter.) It was important for Tisha to focus more on engagement, representation, and action and expression than she had made time for in her earlier years as a teacher. Keeping all students and their needs in mind, she created a classroom culture and workflow that represented a small business rather than a typical classroom. Her motto became "There is *a* way, not *the* way" to remind herself, her colleagues, and her students that there is never only one way to create, learn, execute, or think. Instead of only allowing students to produce work she might imagine, she created space for students to lead themselves to use various methods and strategies to show their learning or thinking process in ways only limited by *their* imaginations. She rejected the one-size-fits-all approach as students were not tied to the traditional classroom floor plan and were given ample choice to practice skills and space to learn self-reflection and feedback.

Implementing leadership ideas is not always easy, as it may take leaders or colleagues time to embrace out-of-the-box thinking. Still, teachers who see the similarities between UDL and college and career environments may start incorporating these strategies gradually and expand as time goes on. Many educators are already approaching their lessons in this manner. If you need some help getting started, the sections that follow offer some detailed ways to create inclusive learning environments that introduce student-led thinking and leadership.

Accessibility

Accessibility is a cornerstone of the UDL approach, and it is essential for creating an environment for all students to participate in their learning experience. Including accessibility in the classroom removes barriers and provides multiple means of representation, expression, and engagement (Meyer et al., 2014).

To achieve this, here are three strategies that cater to diverse student needs, fostering an inclusive learning environment:

- **Media formats:** Students' learning preferences and needs differ. By providing access to various media formats (text, audio, video, interactive media), you can empower your students to consume and create content, as well as communicate their opinions and thoughts in ways that work best for them.

- **Assistive technology:** Screen readers, speech-to-text software, and adaptive keyboards help students with learning challenges gain access and engage in the experience. By implementing assistive technologies, you can ensure students have the necessary tools to partake in learning activities and opportunities.

- **Flexible learning environments:** Crafting a flexible learning environment that accommodates various needs tailors an inclusive environment where all students can feel equal in the classroom. For example, you could adjust your classroom's layout to provide alternative seating options, breakout areas, or safe spaces. All of these can help students focus on their strengths without worrying about what is around them.

Engagement

Capturing students' interests and sustaining their motivation can be enhanced by providing multiple means of engagement in the classroom. UDL emphasizes the importance of engagement and how vital it is to help learners understand the value of their education and leadership roles (Meyer et al., 2014).

To connect students with their learning and sustain motivation, you can implement these engagement-focused strategies:

- **Relevant and authentic learning:** Learning experiences require connecting academic content with real-world issues. When students identify the relevance and authenticity of what they are learning, such as real-world problem-solving, they become motivated to take ownership of their education.

- **Choice and autonomy:** Leadership skills can be developed by choice and a sense of autonomy. To significantly increase their investment and enthusiasm, allow students to choose topics for projects, select roles in a collaborative assignment, or decide how to present their learning. Giving learners control of how and what they do supports their engagement in the classroom and teaches them responsibility for what they own.

- **Inclusive practices:** One of the most important engagement methods is student value. By supporting all students, including those from special populations, you can create a classroom culture that celebrates and values diversity and encourages every student to contribute their unique perspectives and strengths. The world has a million different spaces to explore, and students come to the classroom with the perspective of many of those spaces. Of course, the perspectives will be as vast and different as the students sitting before you. Set up collaborative learning groups and peer mentoring to help build a supportive environment for all to thrive, grow, and develop leadership qualities.

Development of Skills and Abilities

Ensuring a strong foundation for leadership starts with developing a broad range of skills and abilities. It is important to give students varied opportunities to show their learning and build skills essential for their future endeavors.

Here are some ways to implement this idea in the classroom with your students (Kouzes & Posner, 2024):

- **Diverse assessment methods:** Traditional assessment methods, such as standardized testing, often serve only a subset of students and inaccurately reflect the abilities of others. This discrepancy is particularly evident in students who face learning challenges or possess distinct learning styles, highlighting the need for both teachers and students to identify and address these gaps early on. Recognizing this is not just about spotting deficiencies but also about celebrating the diverse ways students express their understanding, ensuring every learner feels valued and seen.

Incorporating varied assessment approaches, such as project-based assessments, presentations, and digital portfolios, enables a richer, more holistic view of a student's abilities. These methods provide avenues to recognize not only academic skills but also creativity, problem-solving, and personal growth. As highlighted in Chapter 2, the AIM Framework reinforces this perspective by encouraging educators to view students as multi-faceted individuals, whose growth is shaped by diverse and overlapping life experiences. By using AIM, teachers can authentically assess and support the individuality and potential of each learner.

- **Focus on soft skills:** Communication, collaboration, and problem-solving skills are more important than ever to incorporate in the day-to-day classroom experience. Soft skills competencies are just as important as academic skills, and align with the UDL Guidelines and the AIM Framework, as well. Activities that promote teamwork, like group projects or peer-led discussions, help students practice the skills that will enhance their confidence and skillset to lead and work with others.

Including soft skills in the academic setting is essential for helping students make connections between the learning environment they are presently in and the tables they will sit at in the future. Those that lack these skills will be at a disadvantage in the job market. According to Mark Perez, a veteran of the service industry as well as a seasoned restaurant and bar lead, "Students today who are entering the workforce are not confident in themselves or their abilities. They have so much doubt and need more affirmation than I have previously seen." Soft skills create a foundation for students to build upon after graduation and support relational leadership characteristics.

- **Feedback and reflection:** Self-reflection helps all of us understand our progress and identify areas for improvement. For students, this is often a missed step in the learning cycle, but it can be a crucial step in connecting them to their learning progress. Regular feedback from teachers, peers, parents, schools, and the community can support growth and development and prepare students for future conversations with bosses, colleagues, or employees. Activities such as journaling, video journaling, blogging, and creating learning portfolios (more about these in Chapter 7) naturally encourage students to think critically about their learning and consider where they have been, where they are now, and where they are going. Practicing this in classrooms as early as possible helps students' development of self-awareness and resilience and gives them an air of confidence they otherwise might not develop until well into adulthood.

Inclusivity and Equity

Inclusivity and equity ensure that individuals have equal opportunities to succeed regardless of their background or abilities (Banks, 2015). One of the downsides of a typical classroom environment is that there are not many opportunities to leave the four walls of the classroom, thus limiting the experiences students have with others from different backgrounds, abilities, preferences, values, and identities. Additionally, when these opportunities are denied, students miss an important chance to learn and practice the Interpersonal Skills and Mastery of Self through the AIM Framework, as described in Chapter 2. By providing fair opportunities for leadership and personal growth, educators can help students develop these essential components to lead with confidence and empathy.

Achieving a meaningful balance between inclusivity, equity, and leadership requires thoughtful action. Here are three strategies that can help make that vision a reality:

- **Equity in opportunities:** Students from special populations may face unique challenges that must be acknowledged and proactively addressed. Providing additional support, like tutoring or counseling, to help these students overcome barriers is a good start, but only the beginning. True equity requires going further by including diverse voices in leadership roles and decision-making processes, ensuring that students from all backgrounds are heard and valued. Additionally, leaders and educators play a critical role in modeling equity by actively demonstrating inclusive practices, such as facilitating open discussions, celebrating cultural differences, and promoting representation within the classroom. By doing so, they set a powerful example and create environments where conversations about equity can thrive. These conversations, involving students, educators, and even the wider community, should focus on understanding and appreciating the diverse experiences and perspectives that each individual brings. Ultimately, this fosters a sense of belonging and mutual respect, paving the way for a truly equitable and inclusive learning environment.
- **Celebrating diversity:** Implementing diverse perspectives into the curriculum and encouraging students to share their cultural backgrounds and experiences creates an

atmosphere that celebrates diversity and helps all students feel valued and respected. Give students voice and choice in how they show their learning. This flexibility enables students to draw on their cultures and background experiences as they create, collaborate, and share.

- **Reducing bias:** We all must strive for fairness and equity in our actions, be open-minded, and be mindful of potential bias in our teaching practices and work. If we guard against bias in assessment methods, classroom interactions, and leadership opportunities, we can ensure that students do not feel excluded or unable to communicate their opinions, even if those opinions are built on their own experience alone.

Implementing Leadership in the Classroom

Before implementing student leadership in the classroom, you must understand each student's strengths and potential. Understanding and embracing student strengths are critical steps toward ensuring you provide leadership opportunities that are aligned with students' abilities and interests. Such opportunities will, in turn, be more relatable and authentic, thereby maximizing each student's potential for success and growth. Once you understand what students are exceptional at, you can shape leadership tasks and assignments that build on those strengths and challenge students to develop new skills. This personalized approach builds confidence, engagement, and a sense of ownership in their leadership roles.

What methods can you adapt to understand student strengths and weaknesses in leadership that aren't too demanding of your available time? Here are a few ideas:

- **Interest inventories and surveys:** At the beginning of the school year, use interest inventories or surveys to gather information about students' hobbies, passions, and preferences. Their responses will help you get a better picture of the personalities and tendencies of your students. Understanding what students are interested in can, in turn, help you identify areas where they might naturally excel or feel more confident taking on leadership roles (Tomlinson, 2001). This could be as simple as a quick survey the first day or week of class asking basic or thought-provoking questions. Incorporating such inventories or surveys throughout the year will help you quickly see students' preferences adapt and adjust as they grow.

- **Strengths-based assessments:** Integrating tools like the CliftonStrengths assessment adapted for younger students (FIGURE 3.1) or other strength-based assessments (such as StrengthsFinder) can reveal individual strengths and provide insights into how each student can contribute to the classroom community (Rath, 2007). This approach allows students to see their assessment results in black and white and begin thinking through past experiences where their strengths and passions radiated.

FIGURE 3.1
The CliftonStrengths four domains of leadership strengths

- **Observations and records:** Regularly observing students in different settings—whole class engagement, group work, independent tasks, and extracurricular activities—is a qualitative approach to gathering data to better support students. You might keep records of interactions, problem-solving approaches, and behaviors. You could then use this data to help identify leadership potential and areas where students naturally take the initiative (Danielson, 2007).

- **Student self-reflections:** Self-reflection activities never fail to engage students, as well as give them an aerial view of their work habits, study habits, language development, leadership, conflict resolution, and so much more! They can record their reflections in written form, in audio form, or on video. Self-reflections could be incorporated into their workflow weekly, monthly, or during the end of each grading period. By utilizing approved digital learning tools, students can document and review their reflections over a period of time, helping them to pinpoint moments where they felt most successful or overcame a struggle and to identify points of growth.

Self-reflections give students insights into their capabilities and specific areas where they can successfully lead (Costa & Kallick, 2008).

- **Peer feedback:** As previously mentioned, incorporate structured peer feedback opportunities during which students can share positive observations, suggestions for improvement, and dialogue about the project or activity. Sharing feedback not only helps students learn how to work within a team-based work environment but also may uncover strengths not immediately visible to teachers and provide students with an additional and broader perspective on their abilities (Topping, 2005).

Integrating one or more of these strategies into lesson designs and students' daily routines will give them a clear picture of their strengths and areas for growth. This allows their path toward success and leadership to come into focus. Also, you, the teacher, get the qualitative data needed to adjust and mold a dynamic learning environment that allows students to try on their leadership hat, maybe for the first time ever. After all, students can lead only if given the opportunity to do so.

Student Leadership Tasks and Assignments

As you grow your understanding of how to "smash" together required learning standards, supplemental standards, and district student profiles, you can begin planning your lessons and activities with each goal in mind. Once you have a clear view of the direction learning will take, you can create activities and opportunities for students to practice and refine their skills. In my classroom, I (Tisha) structured the class and day-to-day activities to resemble that of a small business with students who were grouped into different "departments." For example, students were a part of Customer Service, Public/Educator Relations, or Content Creation in a Principles of IT class where students helped deploy devices, support teachers, and model for students. In a yearbook class, the departments were structured a bit differently to fit our purpose: Editors, Photography, Business Administration, and Sales.

The list that follows offers various strategies you can implement for students that will support them to practice and refine their strengths and weaknesses within leadership. Each strategy requires at least some initial planning, and with consistent implementations and trials, can be altered and shaped to adapt to any classroom environment and support students of all abilities.

▶▶▶ **Rotating leadership roles:** Classroom roles, such as group leader, discussion facilitator, timekeeper, project manager, and technology assistant, could rotate weekly, bi-weekly, or monthly, depending on what suits your environment and culture best. Each student would get the chance to experience different forms of leadership, learn how to connect with classmates or other adults, embrace diverse skills, and build confidence. At the start of each rotation, define the responsibilities and expectations of the roles, as well as provide guidelines and training to help students understand what is required. At the end of the rotation, build in a moment of feedback (with or without digital tools) in which students discuss what they learned from their roles and what could be improved. Receiving feedback from peers and teachers will solidify the purpose and benefit of the experience (Tomlinson, 2001).

▷ *ISTE Student Standards: Empowered Learner 1.1.b, 1.1.c; Knowledge Constructor 1.3.d; Global Collaborator 1.7.b, 1.7.c*

▷ *TLPs: Nurture: Connect Learning to the Learner; Guide: Develop Expertise, Elevate Reflection; Empower: Prioritize Authentic Experience, Ignite Agency*

▷ *AIM Framework: Interpersonal Skills, Mastery of Self*

▶▶▶ **Student-led projects:** The most powerful way to empower and place students in a leadership role is through project-based assignments in which they take the "driver's seat" of learning. This naturally gives them the ability to choose roles that align with their strengths and encourages them to take control of planning, executing, and presenting projects. With an understanding of student strengths and weaknesses, you can guide your class to identify roles that suit them best, provide scaffolding for students to navigate project roles to ensure they have the resources and assistance needed to succeed, and assist with conflict resolution or guidance in overcoming personal obstacles. Students presenting to their peers, school community, or global audiences supports expected learning goals and elevates both the student and teacher beyond the classroom to enhance communication, collaboration, and leadership skills (Larmer et al., 2015).

▷ *ISTE Student Standards: Empowered Learner 1.1.a, 1.1.b; Knowledge Constructor 1.3.a; Innovative Designer 1.4.b*

▷ *TLPs: Nurture: Connect Learning to the Learner; Guide: Spark Curiosity; Empower: Ignite Agency*

▷ *AIM Framework: Academic Excellence, Mastery of Self*

▶▶▶ **Student-led conferences:** A misconception of student-led conferences is that they are time-consuming and unnecessary, especially if educators are focused on successful assessment performance only. Don't believe it. Student-led conferences can support struggling test takers by providing check-in opportunities with students *before* their academic performance gets too low. Student-led conferences help the student with self-reflection *and* help the teacher gain insight into the whole student, which would not occur in a typical memorization-driven learning environment. During checkpoint conferences, students can present academic progress, express struggles they faced, set goals they hope to achieve, and learn how to document their learning process. You could hold face-to-face conferences, but to best document progress try incorporating a written component (via pen and paper or digital documents) to track progress over time. Additionally, this practice allows you to bring parents and administrators into the conversation and confidently show what is working for all students and for individual students.

Remember, empowering students to take an ownership and leadership role in the classroom helps them to gain a deeper understanding of their learning and develop strong communication skills. At the end of each conference, include time for feedback from students. Such opportunities are imperative because they enable students to reflect and to adjust their targets and goals amidst the ebb and flow of progress (Bailey & Guskey, 2001).

▷ *ISTE Student Standards: Empowered Learner 1.1.a, 1.1.b, 1.1.c*

▷ *TLPs: Guide: Spark Curiosity, Elevate Reflection*

▷ *AIM Framework: Academic Excellence, Interpersonal Skills, Mastery of Self*

▶▶▶ **Mini workshops and training:** Skill development allows you to focus on essential skills for your students, such as effective communication, conflict resolution, time management, team building, and decision-making. When creating learning activities around required standards, try incorporating role-playing scenarios, simulations, and group activities, all of which enable students to practice skills in a supportive environment while successfully learning grade-level or curriculum objectives. Furthermore, inviting guest speakers to the classroom to share experiences, read books, participate in question-and-answer forums, and offer insights levels up the learning and leadership for all (Northouse, 2014).

▷ *ISTE Student Standards: Knowledge Constructor 1.3.d; Innovative Designer 1.4.a, 1.4.d; Global Collaborator 1.7.a, 1.7.b, 1.7.c, 1.7.d*

▶ *TLPs: Nurture: Connect Learning to the Learner; Guide: Spark Curiosity; Empower: Prioritize Authentic Experiences*

▶ *AIM Framework: Academic Excellence, Interpersonal Skills*

▶▶▶ **Peer-to-peer mentoring:** Peer-to-peer interactions do not have to be bounded by the walls of a single classroom. There are incredibly powerful ways to incorporate peer activities within a grade level, content area, or across the globe! Some schools have implemented programs or classes where older or more experienced students mentor younger or less experienced peers, providing guidance, support, and leadership where the gap in experience may not be so wide. Matching mentors with mentees is a delicate process as not all matches will be successful. Still, it is important to allow students to experience matches that might not be their first choice to support Mastery of Self and Interpersonal Skills (AIM). Be sure to schedule check-ins between mentors and mentees to monitor progress, receive program feedback, and tackle challenges (Topping, 2005).

▶ *ISTE Student Standards: Empowered Learner 1.1.b, 1.1.c; Global Collaborator 1.7.a, 1.7.b*

▶ *TLPs: Nurture: Ensure Equity; Guide: Elevate Reflection*

▶ *AIM Framework: Interpersonal Skills*

▶▶▶ **Collaborative activities:** Learning activities that require students to work in diverse groups with multiple perspectives afford students the opportunity to assign roles and responsibilities that may be rotated among each other. Collaborative activities support every aspect of AIM, and collaboration is also featured heavily in the TLPs and ISTE Standards. Think through the best way to debrief after each activity to determine benefits and improvements. Consider not just speaking with students yourself but also how students could debrief with each other (Gillies et al., 2008).

▶ *ISTE Student Standards: Empowered Learner 1.1.d; Global Collaborator 1.7.a, 1.7.b*

▶ *TLPs: Nurture: Connect Learning to the Learner; Guide: Develop Expertise; Empower: Prioritize Authentic Experiences, Ignite Agency*

▶ *AIM Framework: Academic Excellence, Interpersonal Skills, Mastery of Self*

▶▶▶ **Extracurricular leadership:** Extracurricular activities, clubs, and sports teams that offer leadership roles can provide additional opportunities for students to develop and practice leadership skills. To help encourage and drive students to take ownership of leadership roles, teachers and schools can acknowledge and celebrate leadership achievements in extracurricular activities within the school community or encourage students to incorporate their extra-curricular interests into learning projects in the classroom. Providing supportive environments that empower students to step into leadership roles outside the classroom greatly prepares them for real-world scenarios (Eccles et al., 2003).

▶ *ISTE Student Standards: Empowered Learner 1.1.b; Knowledge Constructor 1.3.d; Innovative Designer 1.4.a; Global Collaborator 1.7.b, 1.7.c, 1.7.d*

▶ *TLPs: Guide: Develop Expertise; Empower: Prioritize Authentic Experiences, Ignite Agency*

▶ *AIM Framework: Interpersonal Skills, Mastery of Self*

▶▶▶ **Recognition and celebration:** Everyone enjoys being celebrated and recognized, if even briefly. Creating an environment and culture within the classroom where efforts and achievements are regularly recognized and celebrated can lead to students feeling encouraged and valued within the school community. You could, for example, highlight the contributions of student leaders with awards, certificates, special classroom perks, and even a Leader of the Month displayed outside of the classroom. Public recognition during school assemblies, in campus newsletters, at award ceremonies, *and* on social media builds a positive school environment and gives each student leader the sense of belonging.

▶ *ISTE Educator Standard: Leader 2.2.a*

▶ *TLP: Nurture: Ensure Equity*

By introducing some, if not all, of the listed strategies into the day-to-day classroom norms, you can develop a dynamic and inclusive classroom environment where every student can develop, exercise, and refine leadership knowledge. These strategies are meant to enhance individual growth and build a collaborative and empowering educational environment.

The Ripple Effect of Leadership

Imagine a classroom where every student could step into their own power and leadership, where each student was confident enough to take risks with learning, where they saw themselves as a whole individual instead of just a test score, where all skills, abilities, and backgrounds were not just recognized and supported but *celebrated*. Imagine students who could quickly tell you the skills they were most confident in and the ones they were looking to improve without hesitation. It is possible—and it could be yours.

When asked what leadership skills she felt she needed to work on the most, Avery responded, "Asking for help and knowing when to step up or when to take a step back." Her ability to quickly reflect and recognize this illustrates that she had already done a lot of work to reflect on her personal development and had set goals for future improvement. If Avery can do it, your students can too.

We all continue to learn and grow, whether by intention or not. If we model embracing the process of continuous growth to our students and increase and develop our own academic, interpersonal, and self-mastery skills, the natural occurrence will be students who are driven to succeed in the same manner and who discover multiple opportunities to lead. Furthermore, these leadership opportunities encompass the entire spectrum of the learning process: real-world accountability, conflict resolution, communication, critical thinking, problem solving, and adaptability that is reflective, social, and active.

The idea of leadership learning in the classroom is quite frankly the foundation where all else is to be built. Students with a strong sense of self who possess the characteristics of AIM will be more engaged, inquisitive, and curious to seek more information and challenge the status quo. We are all leaders in our own right, and leadership transcends titles or status within an organization. Teachers *are* leaders. Learners *are* leaders. Together they have the power to innovate classrooms, schools, communities, and the world.

tinyurl.com/
TodaysLearners

Scan the QR code to access resources associated with this chapter.

CHAPTER 4

Student Entrepreneurship

Standards and Principles Addressed

The content of this chapter aligns with the following standards, indicators, and principles:

ISTE Student Standards

Empowered Learner (1.1.a, 1.1.b, 1.1.c)

Knowledge Constructor (1.3.d)

Innovative Designer (1.4.a, 1.4.b, 1.4.c, 1.4.d)

Computational Thinker (1.5.a, 1.5.b, 1.5.c)

ISTE Educator Standards

Learner (2.1.c)

Citizen (2.3.a, 2.3.b)

Designer (2.5.b)

Facilitator (2.6.a, 2.6.c, 2.6.d)

Transformational Learning Principles

Nurture: Cultivate Belonging, Connect Learning to Learner, Ensure Equity

Guide: Spark Curiosity, Develop Expertise, Evaluate Reflection

Empower: Prioritize Authentic Experiences, Ignite Agency

Where Teachers Lead, Students Follow

As future leaders, students desperately need the space to think through and discuss the skills they believe they need to confidently navigate, shape, and enhance their thinking process to prepare for an increasingly complex and fast-paced work environment. You may ask, "How can I possibly grow entrepreneurs in my classroom if I am not an entrepreneur myself?" We assure you that you do not need to be a business owner to instill students with this mindset or skill set. In the simplest terms, an entrepreneur is one who undertakes a project or "one who organizes." Teachers are the greatest project managers! Often, teachers manage hundreds of thoughts while also executing half of them into learning projects, communications, or team-building experiences; reviewing and understanding large data sets; and making their visions of student success a reality.

Think of your classroom as an organization that you are leading. When you begin seeing your classroom in this way, you can then start incorporating the skills we discuss in this chapter. To help you better understand what this concept might look like in your classroom, we developed "The Entrepreneur-Driven Classroom Handbook" (FIGURE 4.1). This guide is based on the same handbook Tisha used to create a pitch deck proposing the concept of the unconventional classroom she envisioned. She started with this guide to illustrate the why, what, and *how* to school leaders to get their backing and then continued to adapt and improve it to clearly communicate to students and their parents the purpose of the classroom structure, activities, roles, and responsibilities. Take a close look at Figure 4.1: You will notice the similarities between traditional, entrepreneurial, and business settings and procedures, but a simple change in vocabulary can help students make easier connections between classroom to career. The idea here is that traditional classrooms gradually begin using the vocabulary from an entrepreneur-driven classroom, which would then prepare students for the vocabulary and procedures they will use in the future. (To download this template, scan the QR code at the end of this chapter.)

Creating an entrepreneurial learning environment within the structure of a "typical" classroom environment simply isn't possible. The learning environments we have written about in previous chapters and the environments that still exist today based on the Prussian Model do not serve to create student entrepreneurs. What's your mindset toward incorporating entrepreneurship skills into your learning spaces and classrooms? Using Figure 4.1, take time to think through a few reflection questions to get a better sense of it and what areas you may want to focus on:

TYPICAL CLASSROOM	ENTREPRENEUR DRIVEN CLASSROOM	BUSINESS
Syllabus	Class Handbook	Employee Handbook
Class Rules	Class Core Values	Company Values
Learning Objectives	Class Vision and Goals	Company Vision
Sequence of Courses	Recommended or Related Courses	Professional Development/Learning
Class Behavior/Management	Class and Group Norms	Code of Conduct
Student Information Form	Personality or Behavioral Results	Employee Info & Personality Assessment
Assignments, Exams	Roles and Responsibilities	Job Description
Academic Track	Departments	Departments
Grades and Policies	Performance (rubrics, student-led conferences, grading)	Key Performance Indicators (KPIs)
Acceptable Use Policy (AUP)	AUP/Suggested Productivity Tools	Device, Tech Policy
Classroom Culture	Team Building Events	Employee Perks
Parent Signature	Student and Parent Signature	Employee Signature

FIGURE 4.1

This table illustrates the transformation from a typical classroom to an entrepreneurial classroom that sets students up for real-world skills development.

- How do you balance traditional instructional goals with opportunities to think and act like entrepreneurs?

- How do you currently empower students to identify and explore their passions within your subject area?

- How do you encourage students to embrace failure and to accept the idea of failure as a positive step toward success?

- What type of feedback do you give students to help them improve on their ideas and innovative thinking?

- How do you integrate mentorship, guest speakers, or community involvement to inspire entrepreneurial thinking in your classroom?

- How often are students exposed to leaders in your community or real people using your subject area skills for their current jobs?

The first step, therefore, toward growing entrepreneurs is to reflect on your mindset about incorporating entrepreneurship into your own space. After all, where the teacher goes, the student will follow. Embracing entrepreneurial skills in the classroom and interlacing them with learning standards (e.g., Common Core), supplemental standards (e.g., ISTE Standards, Transformational Learning Principles [TLPs]), and the AIM Framework (Academic Excellence, Interpersonal Skills, and Master of Self) will not only raise the level of learning but also will mold students into leaders who begin thinking of great ideas and solutions to the problems around them. Along the way, they will naturally learn their purpose and begin shaping their personal brand. Each student is unique, bringing different passions, characteristics, and ideas to the table. By leveraging their uniqueness, they can begin to build out their talents and creative solutions.

When thinking of implementing a new idea or strategy in a school district or classroom, it is important to keep in mind that all stakeholders play a key role in the success of the idea. School administrators, like teachers, must reflect on the end goal of student success once again. Buy-in from administrators has the power to fuel students' real-world learning connections to their talents, passions, and purpose. Unwavering support, priority for resources, and trust for teachers play a very important role in closing the gap between the classroom environment and real-world application.

Again, where educators go in their classroom habits, practices, and approaches, students are sure to follow. According to the Waterfall Effect, originated by Paul H. Burton, the benefits and successes (and struggles and weaknesses) of a leader will cascade down into an organization like a waterfall (Graydin, 2022). This leadership principle is applicable to business entities, schools, and school districts across the globe. Whatever discourse or harmony at the top of an organization is sure to trickle down all the way to the students, impacting mindset, learning, confidence, and sense of security. If students are impacted in a negative way, this will directly affect learning, the implementation of AIM, and any additional profiles of success.

As educators, we often boldly tell students, "This is not how the real world will operate." Why, then, are we not creating classroom environments that reflect the modern-day workplace experience? Facilitating an environment for students who can collaborate freely, with varied scheduling to learn adaptability, celebrate success, and embrace imperfections and failures, offers an approach that motivates students and constructs a foundation for strong essential skills such as problem-solving, creativity, communication, and resilience to support a diverse career path.

ESSENTIAL ENTREPRENEURIAL SKILLS FOR STUDENTS

Educators will always play a pivotal role in guiding, inspiring, and supporting students toward developing essential skills for learning *and* for entrepreneurship. But which skills are essential?

We wondered the same thing. Leaning mainly on Rick's experience as an entrepreneur and Tisha's experience implementing entrepreneurship skills with students while meeting career and technology learning standards in her classroom, we listed the most important skills for an entrepreneurial mindset. We reflected on our notes, consulted *The Lean Startup* by Eric Ries and *Entrepreneurship: Theory, Process, Practice* by Donald F. Kuratko, and then reviewed our notes on the AIM Framework. A common thread became clear. These vital entrepreneurial skills align with the same student success goals that are important to *all* stakeholders:

- Vision, Strategy

- Networking, Opportunities

- Financial Literacy

- Operations (productivity, efficiency of process, proper ratio of individuals to responsibilities)

- Leadership, Team Building

- Marketing and Sales Strategies

- Risk Identification ("if, then" rules)

- Innovation and Adaptation

- Legal Compliance and Ethics (Industry Standards, Integrity, Accountability)

- Personal Development

To elevate students to succeed beyond K–12, these skills should be part of students' *everyday* learning and intertwined with district goals for success, the AIM Framework, and additional principles or standards, such as the ISTE Standards and TLPs.

Supporting an Entrepreneurial Mindset in Classrooms

Students begin their learning journey as kindergarteners full of curiosity, imagination, and creativity with little fear of imperfection. By the time they finish middle school and enter high school, they are often filled with fear of their own voice, worry about thinking differently, and have lost the curiosity for being creative in any capacity. It is as if students have been served all their knowledge and thinking on a silver platter by teachers. To guard against this happening in your classroom or school, watch for warning signs by considering:

- Who is doing all the talking in your classroom?

- Who is doing most of the thinking and problem-solving?

- Is the teacher or are the students the most engaged in the learning environment?

- Are students expected to wait for permission to be inquisitive and ask questions?

- Are questions even allowed without control and compliance?

- What norms are being established in your classroom, your school, and your school district?

If students do not feel safe enough to ask questions, they absolutely will not open themselves up to being creative enough to mold their talents and skills into something bigger than the four walls of a classroom. Creativity, leadership, critical thinking, and ideation must be fostered repeatedly and will require room for patience and grace from all stakeholders.

There is an unconscious ideology that students go to school to learn skills they do not have, but once they have entered the heart of the curriculum, the expectations of immediate success and perfect scores become overwhelming, and students then shift their focus from learning to satisfying the expectations of parents, teachers, and school leaders. We cannot expect students to just *know* we are confident in their leadership and ability to succeed. Instead, we need to consciously and intentionally share words and affirm messages to students that encourage growth and unstructured curiosity, and show our belief that they are problem-solvers and have the power to use their voice in ways that create solutions. Behavior is a language, and so it is up to us as educators to foster the belief that students are more than the labels others place upon them and to remind them that we believe in them and their abilities. Over time students will gain confidence in themselves and will step into situations, experiences, and roles they previously avoided. You may see students who previously stayed quiet and never volunteered take the lead on a group project or flourish in building community within your classroom or a school organization. Students who always seemed to be the "sidekicks" or picked last may become the go-to expert for troubleshooting technology. Students who never believed they had anything valuable to contribute may become creators or leaders of school-wide or community-wide projects. Students need help and guidance with personal image and self-development, and when you implement a few small changes to support this you will see a shift in their acceptance of themselves and others. For example, Tisha's former students shared a few messages they received in her classroom that had a lasting impact:

> "Own your shine."

> "You are more than a perfect score or assignment."

> "Your skills and talents are different because they are meant to help others in a different way than your peers."

> "Your voice is powerful, and what you say is what you will see."

> "There is a way, not *the* way."

> "It is okay to take brain breaks. Not every second of your school day must be taken up by thinking."

Equally essential is the encouragement to embrace failure (the lack of an expected outcome from an action) and reframe it as an opportunity for deep understanding and growth. An entrepreneurial mindset knows perfection cannot be achieved the first time around; the path for growth and success is *through* failure. The most crucial step to embracing failure is acceptance (Hreha, 2023), which many students struggle with. As often as possible, remind students (and yourself) that failure is only an event, not a characteristic that defines you. On the flip side, students also must be reminded that perfection does not exist, so it is a waste of time trying to the fit the profile of a "perfect student." Together profiles of success, learning goals, the TLPs, the ISTE Standards, and the AIM Framework can give students a target to aim for, but like a game of darts, hitting the bull's-eye every single time is impossible. Success and failure together create a balanced experience that provides the chance for growth in areas of struggle and empowerment in areas of achievement. In turn, this process creates resilient and adaptable students who become efficient and productive leaders.

Entrepreneurs who build products or offer a service will confirm that a team working together toward a common goal helps to accelerate production and scalable growth.

For a team to work as efficiently as possible, communication and collaboration become vital assets and are critical to the team's success. Communication and collaboration are often two points brought up when assessing improvements in both large and small organizations. These two skills should be introduced and practiced as early as possible. An entrepreneur-driven classroom looks for opportunities where students can practice and refine these skills. Consider your classroom dynamic, and ask yourself:

- Are students engaging in group discussions (in person or online)?

- Do students have a balanced number of individual assignments and group projects? Do the gradebook and year-at-a-glance lesson plans show an imbalance?

- How can lessons and activities better incorporate the practice of speaking, listening, and contributing to a group discussion or topic?

- Are there opportunities for students to illustrate what they have learned?

- Is there a choice available for *how* to show the learning? Are there alternative ways to share and discuss learning in a means that best accommodates student needs?

Asking yourself reflective questions about your teaching practices or classroom set-ups, especially those that have been in place for years, helps you reconsider if you are keeping to a structure just because "it has always been done this way." Adjusting your classrooms to better reflect the future students will enter after graduation can enhance interpersonal skills, cultivate leadership qualities, and leverage the strengths of everyone, including the teacher. To help stimulate entrepreneurial skills, design activities that require students to work together or present to a group, such as to their peers, educators, or the community. Articulating a new idea to someone who has not been involved in its evolution can be difficult, so provide clear and concise explanations to your students and encourage them to do the same in their presentations.

Many students learn by doing, an approach that Rick has always found to be the most impactful for his growth, especially when accommodating his dyslexia in a work environment. Engaging and working with local businesses or community projects gives students a chance at practical experiences and insights into real-world problem-solving, making their learning more meaningful and applicable to real-life scenarios. When students can view and do in a classroom instead of sit and get, the age-old student/teacher script is completely flipped and creates a synergy in the classroom that has students thinking in a different way and teachers facilitating curiosity and communication.

Connecting Learning Standards to Future Jobs

The skills for an entrepreneur cover multiple content areas and can thus be instilled into every single class and subject area. Instead of focusing only on learning standards, think instead about how the standards can fit into the skills your students will take with them after graduation. Consider this process as not a one-and-done solution, but a mindset that should be an expectation for everyone from the superintendent to all support staff. If your shoes are touching the floor of a building where students spend their entire day, your mindset must shift and support their future.

Entrepreneurs wear multiple hats and develop so many skills they are often called a jack-of-all-trades. Students need to understand that they do not have to be "the best" at everything but instead can learn skills that match up with their interests. This might take students on the same journey as an entrepreneur, learning many skills through authentic learning experiences rather than only academics and theory. It is important to note that the number of college enrollments has been declining gradually over the past decade (Fry, 2023) for a few reasons, including avoidance of hefty college bills and of the workplace vulnerability tied to emerging technologies like artificial intelligence (Johnson, 2024). So, in a time when more jobs (excluding STEM-specific careers) are no longer requiring college degrees, experience and skill sets are becoming the greater requirement. Students are now exploring white-collar alternatives, and vocational schools create a straight path to well-paying jobs (Johnson, 2024).

If schools and stakeholders focus only on academic excellence and employers receiving new graduates are more focused on self-mastery and interpersonal skills, how can we support students to find their way into nontraditional career paths? We each need to review which classes, subjects, and projects in our schools and classes already support entrepreneurial skill building and then identify gaps where an entrepreneur mindset could be implemented. This process will be gradual and may start with only a handful of teachers with you leading the focus on future-ready students, but all great change starts with a few people paving the way for a few more.

One way to make the necessary connections to the existing curriculum is to match up the list of essential entrepreneurial skills for students (see the sidebar of the same name) to classes within your school that you believe support similar, if not the same, skills. We brainstormed the shortlist shown in FIGURE 4.2 to get you started but recommend that you plan a roundtable as a collective group with administrators, teachers, and even students to think through how to best pair up courses with the skills in this and previous chapters.

ENTREPRENUER SKILL	CLASSES/SUBJECTS
Financial Literacy	Math, Economics, Career and Technology, STEM, STEAM, Robotics
Vision, and Strategy	ELA, History, Career and Technology
Risk Assessment Identification	Science (hypothesis), Coding/Programming
Legal Compliance and Ethics	Government, ELA
Innovation and Adaptation	Career and Technology, STEM, STEAM, Robotics
Operations, Sales and Marketing, and Sales	Graphic Design, Art, Publishing, Extra Curricular
Leadership, Teambuilding	Extra Curricular, eSports, Student Organizations, Cross-Curricular
Personal Development	Cross-Curricular with learning standards, supplemental standards, and entrepreneurship skills

FIGURE 4.2
Connect classes with entrepreneurial skills.

Personal Branding: The Foundation Development

As students recognize their individual talents and personal skill sets, they begin to build out a story of themselves. Through projects, reflections, and personal development, teachers may be surprised to see students taking their stories and unknowingly building their personal brands. They have grown up watching and relating to influencers on social media who have built their own brands, and in doing so are engaging in a form of microlearning. Brand building *is* a skill that needs to be addressed with our students, at the very least informally. The discussions we have with students in the hallways, during whole group learning, and in one-to-one interactions, for instance, are equally important as direct instruction. Take advantage of these moments to see how students see themselves and their stories.

To better connect learning in the classroom to students' visions of their future, help students learn to share their story, their brand, which will in turn create confidence within them to keep improving and evolving their story and brand. "Personal branding is the overlap between how you see yourself and how others see you" (BerkleyExecEd, n.d.). Just like a company creates a brand to serve as an identity for its products, an individual crafts a personal brand to highlight their unique qualities, skills, and values. The individual (in this case, students) learns how to market themselves and build their learning and career around their story and brand. Students in middle and high school are immersed in social media connections and have learned to be consumers *and* creators while curating their own personal memories (a brand). Their digital footprint becomes their public persona or a living resume that reflects who they are, what they stand for, what they know, and how they can support others. In a sense, a student's brand is created the moment they begin any social profile (with or without adult supervision or permission).

The classroom is a great place to start guiding students' thinking about themselves and their stories. Their online presence (or brand) tells a story as well, including reposts, likes, comments, and original content. Personal branding activities are a great way to combine storytelling with digital literacy and digital citizenship skills. Integrating available technology into students' daily activities will allow students to learn how to effectively use digital tools and devices to leverage a positive online presence (personal brand). Additionally, it will help them better understand how to responsibly use all technology for productivity, creativity, boundary setting, and usage habits. Focusing efforts on what *to* do, instead of what *not* to do, supports students as leaders inside and outside the classroom. Activities such as coding projects, digital presentations, and online collaboration help to build technical skills that students can use to share their stories.

In addition, you might do a brainstorming activity with students and guide them through a brief exercise to begin shaping their personal story. Have them think through the following characteristics in relation to themselves, the energy they bring online and offline, and what makes them uniquely different (Hauwiller, 2019):

- purpose
- values
- clarity
- authenticity
- strengths
- energy
- legacy

You most likely are already addressing these values in your classroom. For example, you share *purpose* with your students daily—the day's learning objectives, schedules, and expected outcomes—so they understand the meaning of the word. Next, you lead them to explore *their* purpose based on their passions and interests. If they are naturally talented with graphic design, for instance, how might that lead them to their purpose in the future? How can they use graphic design to tell their story and create a personal brand? If a student is a gifted public speaker who flourishes in a broadcast class, how can they use that in a positive way to shape their story or digital presence?

Clarity and *authenticity* are usually addressed when teaching students the class norms for speaking in class; asking questions; and locating resources, guidelines, and procedures. Thinking through your course design, projects, and activities, how can they be enhanced or adjusted to allow students to practice using an authentic voice to share aspects of their stories?

Student *strengths* should naturally and organically be identified by the teacher and in turn shared with the student(s), but also, students can utilize the Student Entrepreneur Toolkit (linked in "The Entrepreneur-Driven Classroom Handbook" and discussed later in Chapter 5) to explore this on their own. Doing so will create a culture of discussion and feedback among teachers, students, and peers.

In the book *Unreasonable Hospitality*, author Will Guidara states, "Every person should hear what they did well instead of only what they could do better" (2022, p. 20). In a system where assessments take center stage, mistakes and incorrect answers are the first thing we tend to highlight and discuss with students. What if we were to change the order and instead find ways to show students what they are doing *right*? The identification of students' strengths happens over the course of time and with developed trust between student and teacher or peer to peer.

The energy a student brings to a classroom environment, project, assignment, or assessment is most likely identified early on by teacher and peers. It is hard to dismiss a student loudly acting out upon entering the classroom or constantly complaining about a specific procedure or activity. If a student's energy is off or negative the moment they are seated at their desk or they seem very resistant to an assignment, you need to dive deeper into the cause. You cannot assume students know how to communicate the reason their energy may be off, but you can guide them to articulate a bit of what is going on and help them to become emotionally intelligent over time despite any external circumstances that are causing personal or academic difficulties. Part of a student's growth, and a large portion of the AIM Framework, is personal development, and that includes regulating emotions and the energy they bring to relationships, situations, or environments. You can enlist the help of school counselors or administrators, and once you can get to the heart of an issue (if one is present), you can better help students move into an energy of personal success, one assignment and one day at a time.

Reflecting on "The Entrepreneur-Driven Classroom Handbook," you'll see one of the sections is called "Class Core Values." Giving students time to contribute ideas to a list of class values is a great way to illustrate in real-time what branding and the branding process includes. This is a powerful way to give ownership of the classroom culture and set a foundational mindset for students to take a personal inventory on what values and legacy they want to include as part of their brand. Brainstorming individually or as a whole class might work with a digital mind-mapping tool or with a learning management system's commenting features. Using anonymity and private comments to the teacher only, students are more apt to give their opinions and reasoning on their contributions. Our recommendation is to ask for a maximum of four or five classroom core values. Limiting the aim for students makes it easier to understand and achieve. Tisha's advice is to place the final list of values in places that students look often: next to the learning standards on a whiteboard, on their desks, on their computers, in the class handbook, or as the header of a digital classroom space. Incorporating these values as part of a daily habit will guide students to rewire mindsets about limiting beliefs with learning and their challenges.

In Chapter 7, we will take a more detailed look at some ways students can create a brand around their story with digital portfolios, brand statements, and a social media presence.

Celebrating Success

Often, stopping to celebrate success is something educators neglect to do, but despite what some may believe, it *is* critical to our classrooms. Celebrating students individually or collectively impacts our students far deeper than we educators might anticipate. As university student Annora Elias explained:

> When my achievements are recognized, I feel motivated to continue what I am doing and work harder. When teachers or managers verbally praise me, it feels much more genuine than a printed certificate or being called out publicly in front of peers.
> **—ANNORA**

We may think we simply do not have time for acknowledgment of small victories in our classrooms. We may expect students to just be intrinsically motivated about learning because we are. Some may say, "When I was a student, I did not have anyone celebrating me or my wins. I turned out okay without it, and so will they." Fair point. Some entrepreneurs are ambivalent and skeptical of awards and recognition, but this reveals an internal struggle with self-worth and validation (Clarke, 2023). Educators and school leaders may also have similar feelings surrounding recognition, but just because we struggle with or did not receive celebration of our strengths and triumphs does not mean we should keep those moments from the people we are surrounded by now.

Recognition is not just about external validation, but also about teaching our students and future leaders to take a moment to appreciate the hard work and time spent that led to their accomplishments. As Annora has pointed out, recognition for reaching goals and mastering skills does not cost a thing. Incorporate verbal affirmations throughout your day; model behavior for others to follow with each other and themselves. Successful entrepreneurs know that taking a time-out to recognize themselves, their business, *and* their team fosters a mindset that encourages renewed confidence and self-assurance (Clarke, 2023). In an organizational environment, celebrating achievements might include practices like naming an Employee of the Month or awarding bonuses, gifts, pay raises, or additional paid time off, depending on which fits the receiver best. The motive of recognition should be a morale booster, for the person being celebrated and the entire group, but celebrating achievements may look a bit different depending on the individual or context. For instance:

> I honestly do not think that celebrating success in a typical gen-ed class is very important. I would personally value personal connections with the teacher and students over academic validation. However, in an elective class or class that pertains to a college major, I think it is very important because those classes were chosen because of passion.
> **—ANNORA**

This is a great reminder: Instead of *assuming* we know the best approach for celebration in our classrooms, we all need to take the time upfront to *ask* students what they prefer. Giving them a voice on this topic empowers them and gets us in the habit of giving them a voice to share what works best for them and helps them learn more about themselves and the confidence to share preferences in the future. If you encourage your students, future leaders, to stop for a moment to enjoy the journey of learning as much as the destination, you will teach them the habit of taking time and space to reflect on what went right, what needs improving, and where their goals will take them next.

So, how can you celebrate success in your class? The first thing you need to remember is that celebrating does not need to take up a lot of time or be expensive. What matters the most is *intentional attention*.

Tisha uses several methods for celebrating students; here are a few of her favorite strategies:

- **Video or note encouragement:** Set up an online space for parents or caregivers to record video messages, digital notes, or audio clips to send words of encouragement to their learner. From a fun family lip sync to a heartfelt written list of reasons why they are proud, they can post whatever they feel will resonate with them. You can then share these messages periodically when you spot a student having a bad day or an unforeseen struggle whether personal or academic. After setting up the digital space, mail parents a small blurb about how hard students are working and how much energy they are putting into each of their days with work, extracurricular activities, and the day-to-day, class-to-class workload. Reassure families that even though creating posts of encouragement may be a bit out of their comfort zone, their efforts will provide motivators and reminders to the students that they are seen and valued.

- **Birthday celebrations:** Sometimes a school birthday celebration is the only celebration a student will receive. During your first week of school "get to know you" activities, note how each student likes to be recognized, then apply what you learn to their celebration. For instance, you could put together candy or school supply treats, award certificates, lead a class sing-along, put on a playlist of the class's favorite music, or bestow special privileges during the day or class period. The idea here is not to overthink the celebration. The smallest efforts sometimes make the greatest impact on the student.

- **Newsletter or school announcement shoutouts:** If your school or class has a newsletter, you could recognize a student by running their name and photo (with permission) and even a short paragraph describing the student's achievement! School announcements are a great way to recognize students or student groups across the school community. Both options include recognition from larger groups, such as central administrative teams and family members.

- **Celebration poster:** This group activity costs nothing except about ten minutes of time and a bit of planning. Save it until at least a few months into the school year, however, because it will be more successful once teachers and students have gotten to know each other. Give each student (and yourself) a sheet of paper or cardstock. Have everyone write their name at the top of their sheet and then decorate it as they like. Once everyone finishes decorating, instruct students to each pass their paper to the person to their right, and then to write at least one positive aspect celebrating the student whose name is at the top of the paper they received. Continue passing the posters and writing positive sentiments until everyone has their own paper in front of them again. At the end of the activity, collect the posters, laminate them, and then return them to the owners. This process teaches students to look deeper than just the surface of themselves and their peers and learn to appreciate and give specific feedback to those around them.

- **Shine a light:** When working with students in a whole-class setting, calling on individuals, encouraging students, and encountering struggles with classroom management, you must model to students that there is always something to celebrate about everyone. It's important for you to recognize the greatness in each learner and to vocalize it aloud so the class will embrace each other not just for their similarities but also for their differences. This is mostly a modeling activity because students will mimic your behavior during their interactions with their peers.

A Journey, Not a Destination

Student entrepreneurship skills are not necessarily a single unit of learning, but rather multiple instances, interactions, and conversations over the course of the year(s) you have with students. Create a culture that empowers students to think of learning as a continuous journey rather than a one-and-done destination that ends abruptly at the end of a school day, week, semester, or school year. Celebrate success, connect learning to future jobs, take time to understand and teach personal brand awareness, and lead with an entrepreneurial mindset to create a sense of *belonging*. When people feel they do not belong, their overall performance and well-being will suffer (Cornell, n.d.). We each have an opportunity as leaders of our classrooms to instill a sense of security, support, and inclusion in our student groups. When looking to create a classroom that meets students' needs, Maslow's Hierarchy of Needs gives great perspective. Without a sense of belonging, self-actualization and self-esteem cannot be fully developed or explored (McLeod, 2024).

Mastery of Self (AIM), which includes students' sense of belonging and open-mindedness, is a key factor to begin the shift from a traditional classroom to an entrepreneurial-driven classroom. When you shift your mindset to include the skills discussed in this chapter, your students' mindsets will follow, and they will find themselves thinking more innovatively and creatively when faced with solving problems not obvious to them before.

tinyurl.com/
TodaysLearners

Scan the QR code to access resources associated with this chapter.

CHAPTER 5

Promoting Problem-Solving with Students

Standards and Principles Addressed

The content of this chapter aligns with the following standards, indicators, and principles:

ISTE Student Standards

Knowledge Constructor (1.3.a, 1.3.d)

Innovative Designer (1.4.a, 1.4.b, 1.4.c, 1.4.d)

Computational Thinker (1.5.a, 1.5.b, 1.5.c)

Creative Communicator (1.6.c)

Global Collaborator (1.7.a, 1.7.b, 1.7.c)

ISTE Educator Standards

Learner (2.1.c)

Citizen (2.3.a, 2.3.b)

Designer (2.5.b)

Facilitator (2.6.a, 2.6.c, 2.6.d)

Transformational Learning Principles

Nurture: Connect Learning to Learner, Ensure Equity

Guide: Spark Curiosity, Develop Expertise

Empower: Prioritize Authentic Experiences, Ignite Agency

Why Problem-Solving Matters More Than Ever

During the 2018 "Creative Problem Solving in Schools" study for Adobe, 69% of educators and policymakers said that today's curricula does not place enough emphasis on creative problem-solving and 72% said that education policy is more hurtful than helpful to nurture students' exposure to problem-solving (Adobe, 2018). To support student development of problem-solving skills, educators expressed the need for more training and professional development, control of curricula, and budget increases that prioritize technology and digital tools. What is interesting about this study is that the majority surveyed believed that problem-solving is important for students—and yet the educators who have the authority to prioritize opportunities for problem-solving in the classroom often do not.

The reality for educators and students, which will be no surprise to those veteran teachers reading, is that creating change is up to us. The irony is that *we* must be creative problem-solvers to create an environment that nurtures and supports creative problem-solvers. Students are taught from an early age to wait for the teacher—to give directions, to share knowledge, to identify a problem, to explain how to solve it—and then wait for feedback. Instead, students must be taught and given the opportunity to practice defining a problem. Problems outside of the classroom are unstructured and unpredictable. Inside the classroom, problems have been well thought-out by the teacher or guided by required curriculum or standards and hardly mimic real-world environments.

The World Economic Forum lists analytical thinking as a top skill and an urgency for reskilling and filling gaps with training among employees (Whiting, 2020). If students complete high school, earn a college degree, and enter the workforce as an employee or entrepreneur without analytical and problem-solving skills, then it becomes the responsibility of the companies they work for to create opportunities for continued learning and reskilling. Although this poses a major problem for companies, it is even more of a problem for the student, who is suddenly thrust into the adult world of problem-solving. If they have never been expected to learn to think through problems and solutions, how can we expect them to just know how? If we do not offer them guidance and scenarios that require them to "put their thinking caps on," the responsibility will then lie on them to catch up once they graduate.

To better equip ourselves to lead our students, we must be able to identify what problem-solving is, why it is important, how to introduce it, and how it specifically benefits everyone involved. This chapter will guide you through several problem-solving frameworks you can use as a starting point, as well as offer practical examples and strategies for implementing simulations in the classroom.

Problem-Solving Frameworks

Problem-solving frameworks provide a structured methodology that guides one or many problem-solvers through a series of steps helping to identify, analyze, and resolve problems effectively and efficiently (Karami, 2023). There are numerous recognized frameworks that offer unique perspectives that may be tailored to different types of problems, whether they are simple, complex, theoretical, or practical. For this reason, not every framework will necessarily support the requirements needed to solve the problems that entrepreneurial leaders may face. If an entrepreneur is building a software company, for instance, a framework like the scientific method, which involves hypothesis-driven inquiry and empirical testing, may not be as well suited to the problem as design thinking or Six Thinking Hats. Therefore, rather than adhering to a single "best" framework, you must assess a framework to ensure it fits the process of solving the problem at hand.

Implementing problem-solving frameworks in the classroom establishes a solid foundation for the learning process, providing students structured strategies to tackle challenges. These frameworks serve as both visual and practical tools, enabling students to connect the skills they develop to real-world scenarios. By consistently demonstrating how these methods can be applied to future academic, professional, and personal contexts, you help students build confidence and address the common question, "How is this going to help me in real life?" This approach equips students with a replicable process for analyzing and resolving problems, fostering critical thinking, and preparing them for diverse scenarios beyond the classroom. Ultimately, this leads to stronger decision-making skills, a key component of the Mastery of Self component of the AIM Framework.

One of the biggest challenges for high school and middle school students is becoming overwhelmed by a problem, task, or project, and then just freezing because they do not have the skill set to overcome the feeling. Often students have not practiced the art of problem-solving enough, at no fault of their own, and those missed opportunities can silently contribute to feelings of anxiety, issues with self-worth or confidence in learning—just ask Juli Parsons.

> Most of the time when I felt like I was stuck in a problem, it was because I had decision fatigue. I felt so overwhelmed or exhausted by all the things I had already tried or completed that it was difficult for me to pick a forward moving path.　**—JULI**

In a world where students are constantly having to face extremely challenging circumstances like bullying, unsupportive or major shifts in relationships, change in family dynamics, or the natural progression of developing hormones, it is common for students to feel overwhelmed before their feet even enter our classrooms or schools. The circumstances they bring with them as they sit at their desks are often completely out of their control. So, when it is time to focus on academics, they are often not confident in their ability to solve the challenges they face in the classroom. This is where the opportunity lies to show them, teach them, and model problem-solving skills that include reflective moments where students can safely practice how to approach small and large problems in their path. Implementation of daily problem-solving provides students with authentic and real-world learning moments by *doing* instead of only *hearing* of the benefits. For educators to lead students to lead themselves, it is important to take time to study the possible frameworks that best suit students.

Frameworks to Support Leaders

Of the numerous frameworks available to learn and apply, some are a better fit for student leaders and others are more suited to entrepreneurs. Benjamin Hamilton, a twenty-year-old University of Texas junior majoring in advertising, explained:

> The biggest difference in solving problems now compared to when I was in school is my peers and I have had to learn idea generation *after* leaving the K–12 environment. Of course, we learned mind-mapping in school, but now I implement design thinking, an idea I was never introduced to during middle or high school. When these methods are used with the ability to really practice it, you never have to go back to study it. Finding my passion and learning how to use it to my advantage without being told has been powerful. Everything I need to learn is out there if I take the initiative with learning instead of waiting for my teachers or professors.　**—BENJAMIN**

Frameworks have become more valuable today than ever before, so here are three frameworks that we believe can be implemented easily in the classroom and that students will be successful at incorporating into their day-to-day activities.

The Six Thinking Hats Method

Developed by Edward de Bono, the *Six Thinking Hats* framework is a decision-making and problem-solving method. Adaptable for both individual learners and groups, it encourages those involved to approach problems, meetings, and issues with six distinct perspectives, represented by six colored hats: White, Red, Black, Yellow, Green, and Blue (FIGURE 5.1; for a color version of this image, scan the QR code at the end of the chapter to access this chapter's resources). Each hat signifies a particular type of thinking, allowing individuals to focus on one specific aspect of a given problem at a time:

- **White hat:** Represents information gathering such as data analysis and fact-finding. White hat thinks about the knowledge and insights collected but also will point out what is missing and work out how to retrieve it.

- **Red hat:** Represents emotions, feelings, and vibes. Red hat uses instincts and intuition. This hat approaches problems with more emotion and often expressively without justifying reasoning with logic.

- **Black hat:** Represents caution and critical judgment and is often used to predict negative outcomes. Black hat assesses potential risks and explains concerns about a specific solution.

FIGURE 5.1
The Six Thinking Hats framework

The Six Thinking Hats

The white hat
Data, facts & information
What we know, and what we ought to find out

The blue hat
Manages the process
Listens, directs attention, integrates, moves forward

The yellow hat
Sunshine & positivity
Optimism, possibilities, upsides, potential

The red hat
Feelings, reactions & vibes
How we feel: gut instincts honest emotions, intuition

The green hat
Creativity & surprise
Alternatives, reframing, out-of-the-box ideas, what-ifs

The black hat
Caution & skepticism
Dangers, threats, risks, drawbacks, worst-case scenarios

- **Yellow hat:** Represents optimism and positive thinking. Yellow hat naturally opposes Black hat's approach to problems because Yellow hat highlights the benefits, usefulness of solutions, added values, positive aspects, and opportunities.

- **Green hat:** Represents creativity and new ideas. Green hat thinks about potential ideas and alternatives, using outside-of-the-box thinking to explore potential ways forward.

- **Blue hat:** Represents process, control, and organization. Blue hat is focused on managing which decisions need to be made, ensuring an agenda is maintained, documenting summaries, and keeping to the agreed upon action items.

The Six Thinking Hats method helps to reduce bias, enhance creativity, balance emotion and logic, and identify risks and benefits (de Bono, 1999). It is also perfect in group settings (group projects or collaborative activities), ensuring that all voices are heard and all aspects of a problem are considered. Additionally, it helps students to see differing perspectives of an issue in a more structured way and allows them to explore a different way of thinking if only for a moment.

Design Thinking

Design thinking is a mindset and approach to problem-solving and innovation focused on human-centered design (Han, 2022a). Many of the top companies in the world use the design thinking approach for innovation and ideation because it is solution-based instead of problem-based (Han, 2022b). Rather than focusing on just the problem and losing valuable productivity time, design thinking focuses on providing meaningful and impactful solutions to a problem, challenges assumptions, redefines problems, and helps create more innovative solutions.

While within a business context design thinking often focuses on finding solutions that best serve client and customer needs, students can use the five stages of the design thinking process to problem-solve as well:

1. **Empathize:** Students observe, engage, and immerse themselves in a situation to understand needs, desires, and challenges empathetically. They can conduct interviews, create questionnaires, and make real-time observations to gain a clear understanding of the bigger picture.

2. **Define:** Using insights gathered in the Empathize stage, students identify the core problem they want to address. This step helps them clarify the challenge and focus their efforts on finding meaningful solutions.

3. **Ideate:** Students unleash their creativity and curiosity by generating a wide range of ideas to solve the defined problem. Activities like brainstorming, sketching, and mind mapping encourage free thinking and help them confidently visualize potential solutions.

4. **Prototype:** Students create simplified versions of their ideas from the Ideation stage. These can include sketches, mock-ups, or models that give enough detail to explore whether an idea could work as a solution.

5. **Test:** Students implement and refine their prototypes, gathering feedback to improve the solution. Testing encourages them to observe how their ideas perform and to iterate based on what they learn to achieve the best possible outcome.

The design thinking process is a continuous loop that does not always go in the same order, however. Students bounce back and forth from the Define stage to the Prototype stage multiple times, or even return to the Empathize stage, before a solution eventually emerges. Through this process, students learn that a problem may have multiple right answers and that perfection is a myth that can never actually be achieved.

If you research design thinking further, you may find several variations of the stages and their names. Tisha's advice is to home in on the stages themselves using wording that would make sense for your learning environment and students. You know your students best and know how to frame knowledge in a way that makes sense to them. For example, Tisha described the design thinking stages to her students as Define the Problem, Possible Solutions, Steps/Process, Implement, and Improve (FIGURE 5.2). This personalized approach made sense for students, and Tisha gave them a bit of ownership in which words resonated with them when introducing the process. Doing so helped make everyone comfortable referencing the process daily when solving problems and when Tisha guided students toward answers to their questions during open-ended inquiry-based projects, group activities, and even with conflict resolution.

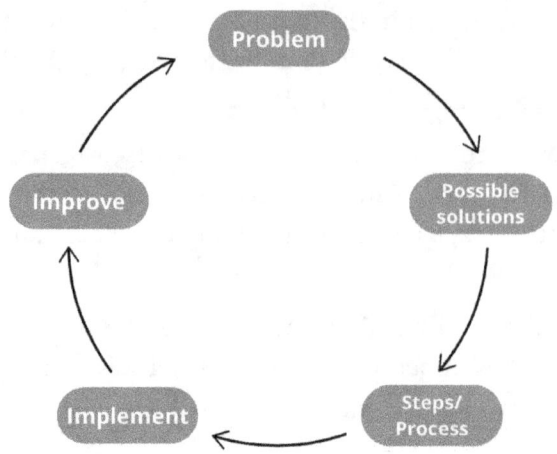

FIGURE 5.2
Design thinking is a
continuous circle of
innovation (Problem,
Possible Solutions,
Steps/Process,
Implement, Improve),
repeating to refine
and evolve solutions.

SWOT Analysis

SWOT analysis is a strategic planning tool used to identify and analyze the internal and external factors that can impact the success of a project, organization, or business venture. SWOT, which stands for Strengths, Weaknesses, Opportunities, and Threats, helps organizations understand internal capabilities and external environments. This framework guides students to develop ways to leverage their strengths, acknowledge and improve areas of weakness, find the confidence to say yes to great learning opportunities, and anticipate threats or possible struggles. The SWOT problem-solving framework is versatile yet simplistic, making it a great solution for students to understand and apply as they transform personal development (FIGURE 5.3). Take a closer look:

- **Strengths:** Focus on student strengths, natural skills and talents, and ways that differentiate them from others.

- **Weaknesses:** Reflect on what might be an obstacle to completing assignments or projects, consider where improvements can be made, and identify what the student can control versus what is out of their control.

- **Opportunities:** Create opportunities for student growth with lesson design; stretch their thinking with projects that have them relying on a different perspective; and encourage them to take small, calculated risks with school activities or hobbies.

- **Threats:** Guide students to anticipate threats or possible struggles and know which external factors (school or non—school related) might impact or set them back from their goals.

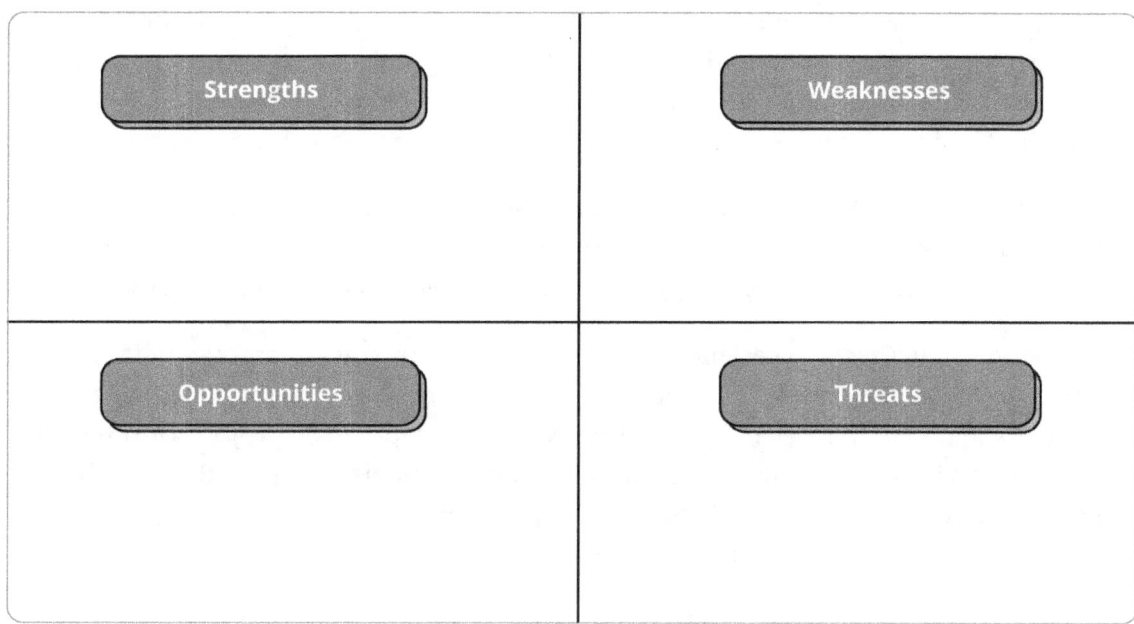

FIGURE 5.3
An example SWOT analysis template

Using the Right Method

After learning about three possible problem-solving frameworks for students, you're probably pondering which approach is best to implement with your students or which will help them most to become comfortable and successful with problem-solving. Remember what we said about design thinking and problems having more than one solution? The same is true here. The best-fit framework may differ from class to class or as you evolve your teaching practice. To begin, we recommend:

1. Consider the frameworks in this chapter, as well as any others you are already familiar with, and commit to gradually implementing a framework into your curriculum and day-to-day classroom operations.

2. Pick one framework (or a combination of two) that you feel comfortable with and understand easily. The more comfortable you are with your choice, the more confident you will be when discussing it with your students and parents.

3. Apply the framework to the classroom culture, daily activities, and major projects. The goal here is to get students familiar with the idea of problem-solving and integrate the process as part of the expectation of learning. This can be pivotal for future experience, as Annora Elias has seen firsthand:

> I think that [problem-solving] can be practiced through examples and doing. For example, during one of our team meetings at work, my manager would give us customer scenarios to work through as if we were selling to someone. **—ANNORA**

4. Follow through. Create experiences and moments for students to practice what they have watched and learned. This step involves being open to constant dialogue with students to understand their logic and approach to completing a project, working out challenges with group dynamics, or deciding the best elements to add to a learning portfolio as they move on to college or job applications.

A Journey to Transformative Problem-Solving

Tisha had a vision for her classroom: She wanted her students to see beyond the immediate goal of completing assignments, receiving a grade, and obtaining a high school diploma. She realized many struggled to connect cross-curricular learning and adapt new knowledge to the real world they lived in as well as the future that awaited them. This was a problem Tisha set out to solve.

Determined to make a change, Tisha used two powerful frameworks: SWOT analysis and design thinking. These frameworks became essential tools in her strategy to help students develop problem-solving skills, critical thinking, and a forward-looking perspective.

Building the Student Entrepreneur Toolkit

To support her students' journey, Tisha created the Student Entrepreneur Toolkit (FIG-URE 5.4). This resource was designed to help students document their progress over time, offering templates for goal-setting, reflective prompts, and space to analyze their growth. At the beginning, Tisha introduced SMART goals to her students and taught them how to set specific, measurable, achievable, relevant, and time-based goals relevant to their lives to give them a bit of control and a foundational framework to build upon later for deeper learning with problem-solving frameworks.

What are SMART goals?		
SMART goals are a way to make sure the goals you set are clear and easy to follow. Each letter in the word "SMART" stands for something important to help you reach your goals. This practice will help you improve academic excellence, interpersonal skills and mastery of self.		
To practice using SMART goals, pick 1-3 goals and fill each each section. Review these each week or month.		
S(pecific)	Your goal should be clear and not too general. You need to know exactly what you want to achieve.	Example: Instead of saying, "I want to get better grades," say, "I want to get a B or higher in math this semester."
M(easurable)	You should be able to measure or track your progress so you'll know when you've achieved it.	Example: "I want to read 10 pages of my book every day," instead of just saying, "I want to read more."
A(chievable)	Make sure your goal is realistic. It's great to challenge yourself, but it shouldn't be impossible.	Example: "I'll run a mile without stopping by the end of the month," is achievable if you practice a little every day.
R(elevant)	Your goal should be important to you and fit with what you care about or need to do.	Example: If you love sports, a relevant goal might be, "I want to practice shooting basketball for 30 minutes every day."
T(ime-bound)	Give yourself a deadline so you know when to finish your goal.	Example: "I want to memorize 20 vocabulary words by next Friday."

FIGURE 5.4

The Student Entrepreneur Toolkit Tisha used with her students

Students were given autonomy on how to use the toolkit in the format that suited them best; some preferred to jot notes on printed templates, whereas others kept digital records. The idea of the Student Entrepreneur Toolkit was to prepare students for the implementation of student-led conferences (discussed later in Chapter 7). The strategy was to get students in the habit of showing evidence of learning, self-reflection, and solution-oriented discussions. The SWOT framework helped students evaluate their strengths, weaknesses, opportunities, and obstacles. This reflection practices self-awareness, enabling students to identify areas for growth and plan actionable steps. By regularly engaging with these processes, students develop a sense of agency and responsibility for their own learning. You can download the Student Entrepreneur

Toolkit to assist you with your own implementation of problem-solving strategies; simply scan the QR code at the end of the chapter.

Embedding Frameworks into Daily Practice

Tisha knew that to truly prepare her students for the future, problem-solving needed to be woven into their everyday routines. To achieve this, she used visual cues in the classroom, displaying strategies like design thinking, weekly class and individual goals, and key learning objectives. By consistently referencing the visuals, Tisha modeled problem-solving behaviors, showing students how to reference the strategies with small or large scenarios, break tasks into manageable steps, and connect their daily work with larger goals (FIGURE 5.5).

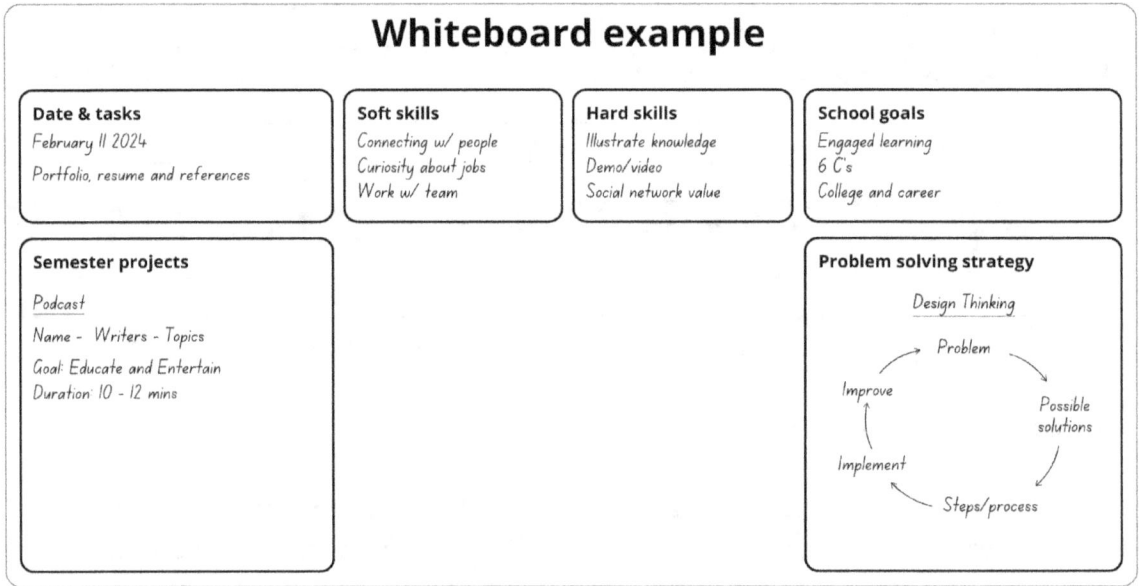

FIGURE 5.5
An example of a whiteboard Tisha would prepare for her students

Over time, students began to internalize these habits, applying problem-solving frameworks not only in the classroom but also in extracurricular activities and personal pursuits. They started seeing connections across subjects and recognizing how these skills could prepare them for a dynamic, ever-evolving future.

Bridging Classroom Learning with Future Readiness

Tisha's approach, deeply rooted in the ISTE Student Standards and Transformational Learning Principles (TLPs), emphasized critical thinking, collaboration, and creativity. This strategy not only fostered academic excellence and interpersonal skills but also encouraged students to take ownership of their learning, helping them develop the qualities of Mastery of Self outlined in the AIM Framework:

- Self-reliance and confidence grew as students used the Student Entrepreneur Toolkit to reflect on their progress and plan for improvement.

- Decision-making and goal-setting were strengthened through SMART goals and structured problem-solving activities.

- Regular engagement with reflective practices fostered self-awareness and a growth mindset, preparing students for lifelong learning and adaptability.

Through this approach, Tisha transformed her classroom into a hub for future-ready learning. Her students didn't just complete assignments; they built the skills, mindset, and resilience to navigate real-world challenges and succeed in their future careers.

By empowering her students with practical tools and fostering independence, Tisha ensured that they were not only prepared for academic success but also equipped to thrive in a complex, ever-changing world.

Problem-Solving, the 4 Cs, and Leadership

Problem-solving skills, leadership skills, and the 4 Cs of education encompass a wide array of transferable skills for students from the classroom to the workplace. Identified in 2004 by the National Education Association's Partnership for 21st Century Skills, the four foundational Cs of education are:

- Critical thinking
- Communication
- Collaboration
- Creativity

Problem-solving in the classroom encompasses all the foundational Cs, and problem-solving frameworks lead students to learn strategic curiosity and the art of question asking to clarify understanding, begin finding solutions to problems, and learn how to best lead themselves and others. A student's K–12 learning journey can diminish their opportunity or motivation to ask questions. Over the course of time, more focus is given to "teaching for the test" and less to learning how to ask questions to find possible solutions. Simply put, students are not learning *how to learn*. Learning includes many of the key components of the problem-solving frameworks, including active listening, communication of ideas, reflection, goal setting, finding relevance, and asking questions. Understanding how best to formulate questions is a key step in learning how to think. In John Maxwell's *Good Leaders Ask Great Questions* (2014), he states, "If you want to be successful and reach your leadership protential, you need to embrace asking questions as a lifestyle" (p. 4). If you want your students to become great leaders, you must create an inquiry-based culture that supports their curiosity, creativity, and questions, as well as model positive dialogue. If you do, when they enter a professional setting, they will be equipped with the confidence to ask the right questions, articulate follow-up questions, collaborate on possible solutions, and clearly understand action items. Questioning makes us all better at resolving issues and refining solutions. When we take time to model and teach this with students, we validate the idea that they have what it takes to become brilliant leaders.

To guide students in forming good questions, ask your own. Introduce and model questions that focus on active listening like "This is what I heard you say, did I get that right?" or use follow-up questions that affirm student voices like "You're sharing some incredible thoughts, and I don't want to miss it, can you repeat that?" Think of questions that focus on elaboration, clarification, outcomes, perspectives, planning, and predictions. Model questioning in groups when introducing a new topic or lesson; add unit-related questions to digital tools students use; or model inquiry during group projects, assignments, activities, and self-reflection. To assist you and your students on how to ask better questions, we created the "Good Leaders Ask Good Questions" document; scan the QR code at the end of the chapter to access it. To tie leadership, problem-solving and the 4 Cs together, think of how best to layer or combine each component to lesson design, student activities, and project-based learning. Over time, scaffold the process so students can become confident in their own skills and processes.

Leveraging Emerging Technologies

Over the last fifteen to twenty years, technologies have evolved and revolutionized how students access, consume, and analyze information. Emerging technologies are still changing and adapting to the educational landscape, and many can support problem-solving skills. We must embrace these new tools now to prepare students because there is a high probability these technologies will be used in their future careers. Trying something new can be a motivator to learning, so here are some emerging technologies to investigate:

- **Artificial intelligence (AI):** Since 2022, AI has exploded within educational communities, as has the emotionally fueled debate around this technology. Some educators are completely resistant to the idea of using AI themselves or with students, whereas others foresee AI's potential for improving productivity and efficiency. School or district policies are needed to keep students' data safe, but AI also has the potential to aid students by offering adaptive learning or tutoring based on a student's performance, adjusting the difficulty at a speed that is suitable to the student. Additionally, AI can create real-world examples, immediate feedback, and tailored hints to guide students through the process of problem-solving while accelerating the learning progression. Furthermore, AI can be used to help students practice key learning standards such as writing prompts, responses, critically thinking, vetting and validating resources, and research.

- **3D printing:** Giving students the ability to create physical objects from digital models, this technology bridges the gap between concept and reality. With the inclusion of geometry, functional requirements, and material properties, 3D printing can offer more complex problem-solving scenarios and prototyping for design thinking. Students can practice problem-solving strategies, such as answering difficult questions, thinking through and planning a budget, using ideation, and discovering that mistakes cost money—not to mention they'll learn how the printer and associated software work.

- **Robotics:** Involving design, building, and programming, robotics provides students with a multidisciplinary learning experience to solve a specific problem. Students could be required to collaborate, divide tasks, communicate effectively, and combine their efforts to create a functional robot to complete a set of requirements. Their creation then could be tested in competition settings organized by state education organizations, independently owned businesses, or non-profits. By introducing robotics as a portion of the curriculum or creating extracurricular opportunities, we help to simulate real-world engineering challenges, iterative problem-solving, and creatively strategic solutions for students.

- **Extended reality (XR):** Artificial reality (AR) and virtual reality (VR) immerse students in a simulated environment, enhancing a student's experience to solve problems in a controlled and risk-free space. STEAM educators can take full advantage of extended realities like visualizing human anatomy, dissecting an animal, disassembling an engine, and 3D painting or modeling. Very few, if any, students will have real-life encounters with scenarios such as these. However, extended reality (XR) moves students one step closer to a more realistic environment, where they can practice hands-on skills, analyze and immediately see where they have missed the mark, and find potential solutions to success.

- **Internet of Things (IoT):** The Internet of Things can be found in our day-to-day activities: smartwatches, smartphones, laptops, tablets, and smart home devices. IoT projects often require knowledge of coding, electronics, and data analysis. Understanding the foundations of these devices—how they were designed and how they work—facilitates problem-solving and troubleshooting, improves student communication with other users, and helps them make decisions based on data and patterns.

Emerging technologies offer innovative and interactive ways to cultivate problem-solving skills that most standard classroom environments cannot provide. By leveraging cutting-edge tools, educators can create more effective learning spaces that nurture critical thinking, creativity, and adaptability. These technologies engage learners, while also preparing them for more complex problem-solving tasks in the future. To dive deeper and expand your knowledge of emerging technologies, check out two ISTE-published books by Rachelle Dené Poth: *How to Teach AI: Weaving Strategies and Activities Into Any Content Area* (2024) and *What the Tech? An Educator's Guide to AI, AR/VR, the Metaverse and More* (2025).

The Start of a Strong Foundation

No matter what we teach, who we teach, or when we teach, problem-solving skills are the cornerstone for learning, leadership, and entrepreneurship, and they're essential to any lesson, activity, or project we choose to implement with students. As educators, we know best how to design our classrooms and lessons so that problem-solving can be interwoven into every inch of our classroom and included in all interactions and conversations. Instead of creating a single lesson that teaches problem-solving or limiting students' exposure to inquiry-based learning to one or two elective classes, we *must* find and continuously search for creative ways to teach students the skills today that they will need tomorrow. We cannot continue expecting others to make these skills a priority. As an employer, restaurateur Wilborn Blalock understands the consequences of this inattention all too well:

> 75% percent of the new employees I hire have no clear knowledge of true work ethic, drive, or how to be a team player understanding the consequences of their real-life actions. Hiring people who have never been employed, lack problem-solving skills, are unsure of how to positively interact with people, or who have never learned conflict resolution makes my job as a business owner ten times more difficult because I must teach them so much more than the day-to-day operations. Students need to learn early on to move and act with purpose, have practiced the best ways to connect with people, ask questions, and be curious. Ideally, students would come to me expecting to be prompted to solve their own problems and with a work ethic rooted in the idea that if you're going to do something, approach it with the intent of doing it well.

For all grades and classes, foundational problem-solving skills are a requirement for building future-ready students. Missing these can impact aspects of students' lives in ways that educators may never be able to see. We each have the power to be intentional and help students find their passions. Teaching them how to learn without being forced or told can give them an undiscovered sense of empowerment, but not doing so is a disservice to our future leaders.

tinyurl.com/
TodaysLearners

Scan the QR code to access resources associated with this chapter.

Innovative Thinking:
The Cornerstone of Authentic Assessment

Standards and Principles Addressed

The content of this chapter aligns with the following standards, indicators, and principles:

ISTE Student Standards

Empowered Learner (1.1.a)

Knowledge Constructor (1.3.a, 1.3.b, 1.3.c, 1.3.d)

Innovative Designer (1.4.a, 1.4.b, 1.4.c, 1.4.d)

Computational Thinker (1.5.b)

Creative Communicator (1.6.a, 1.6.b, 1.6.c, 1.6.d)

Global Collaborator (1.7.c, 1.7.d)

ISTE Educator Standards

Learner (2.1.b, 2.1.c)

Leader (2.2.b)

Collaborator (2.4.b)

Designer (2.5.a, 2.5.b, 2.5.c)

Facilitator (2.6.a, 2.6.c, 2.6.d)

Analyst (2.7.c)

Transformational Learning Principles

Nurture: Connect Learning to Learner, Ensure Equity

Guide: Spark Curiosity, Develop Expertise

Empower: Prioritize Authentic Experiences, Ignite Agency

Life: Not Just A Memory Game

Traditional student assessments, like standardized tests and completion-only work, fail to capture the true authenticity of students' abilities. Students are essentially tested on how good their short-term memory is with large volumes of information or on how to complete a task for which they focus on a final product, rather than the learning experience from beginning to end. This surface-level engagement with the content means students will aim to meet only the minimum requirements to complete a task or pass a test. As a result, the information that they consume will most likely be forgotten soon after the test and never be recalled or applied again. These approaches undermine the learning process and fail to encourage a deeper understanding of each subject (Pellegrino & Hilton, 2012).

Reflecting on his own experience at school and evaluating the process of how he was assessed, Rick sometimes wonders, "Did I learn to understand, or did I learn to pass a test?" Ask the same question of many former (or current) students, and they would likely confess that their primary goal was (or is) to get a high grade or at least pass the test and class rather than truly understand the content and why it is important. For Rick, subjects like English, Chemistry, and History often felt like a memory exercise rather than a meaningful learning opportunity. He would memorize facts and complete homework, only to recall the material for an end-of-year test, but never with the intention of retaining the information for future use. Juli Parsons echoed Rick's thoughts when asked if she felt that middle school and high school tests reflected what she learned, saying:

> I feel that tests were more a reflection of my ability to retain short-term information, and of course, there were plenty of classes that required the ability of memorization.
> —JULI

This instructional approach is not a true measure of understanding, but instead an evaluation of short-term memory capabilities. Unless we are aiming to teach our students how to become actors, whose key skills include memorizing and delivering lines, the approach of consuming and memorizing information without understanding its context offers little benefit.

For most learners, the challenge lies in finding the connection between what they are learning and how it connects to the real world. If we cannot bridge the gap between academia and reality, students will never understand why they are required to know certain information to graduate. This lack of understanding often causes a lack of intrinsic motivation and apathy. The disconnect between the classroom and the outside world creates a perception that students are not capable of leading or learning. Therefore, it is important to shift the educational strategy from a fixed and structured learning environment to one that balances structure with flexibility. Specifically for student assessment, flexibility over rigidity becomes vital when transitioning to more personal and authentic evaluations. Authentic assessments should focus on knowledge and skills in real-world scenarios and promote deeper understanding and long-term retention of information.

In this chapter, we will define innovative thinking and explore how it lends itself to authentic assessment of student performance. By embracing innovative thinking, we can expand beyond the limitations of standardized tests to create assessments that reflect a student's competence and ability to apply their learning to solve problems that matter.

Understanding Innovative Thinking

Innovative thinking is the ability to approach challenges, problems, and opportunities with a creative and forward-looking mindset. It involves generating new and original ideas, questioning established norms, and finding novel solutions to complex issues (Alam, 2024).

Innovative and critical thinking can transform traditional teaching and learning and inspire adjustments to current pedagogy, curriculum delivery, and learning environments. To embrace innovative thinking during lesson planning and design is a step toward preparing students for future challenges and equipping them with the necessary skills to navigate and thrive in any challenge they may face.

A key aspect of innovative thinking is the attention to personalized learning. *Personalized learning* is a tailored approach that considers a student's characteristics, preferences, and needs to enhance their learning outcomes effectively and efficiently (Shemshack & Spector, 2020). With the use of data and technology, you can create custom sets of instructions tailored to an individual student's needs, enhancing engagement and improving learning outcomes. The shift from a one-size-fits-all approach helps foster a wider range of personalized experiences, such as adaptive learning technologies, adjusting content and pace based on a student's performance, and project-based learning that allows students to explore topics that are of interest to them.

Another critical part of innovative thinking is bridging the gap between academia and reality, which is vital for authentic assessment of students. By connecting classroom learning with real-world problems and experiences, you can bring relevance and depth to your teaching. For instance, in a unit about sustainable agriculture, partner with local farms to give students hands-on experience planting crops, learning about eco-friendly farming techniques, and understanding supply chains. Similarly, for a project on urban planning, you might collaborate with a city planning department to involve students in designing solutions for traffic congestion or creating green spaces.

Partnering with local businesses, community organizations, or nonprofits can provide valuable work experience and opportunities for engaging field trips that immerse students in real-world environments. These experiences offer context and relevance to classroom lessons and spark curiosity to further expand students' understanding of the subjects they study.

Bridging the gap between theoretical concepts and practical applications helps students learn to combine knowledge and ideas across the curriculum and apply them in all aspects of their lives. This approach aligns closely with the principles of the AIM Framework (Chapter 2):

- **Academic Excellence:** Through real-world learning experiences, students engage in critical thinking, problem-solving, and creative expression, which are hallmarks of Academic Excellence. They are empowered to take ownership of their learning while collaborating globally and analyzing information to address complex challenges.

- **Interpersonal Skills:** These experiences coincide with Interpersonal Skills like effective communication, collaboration, leadership, empathy, and inclusivity. Students learn to work with diverse perspectives and develop a service-oriented mindset, preparing them to thrive in interpersonal and professional contexts.

- **Mastery of Self:** By navigating real-world challenges, students develop Mastery of Self, cultivating self-reliance, resiliency, confidence, and self-discipline. They reflect on their experiences to set meaningful goals and approach problems with open-minded curiosity and persistence.

This holistic approach prepares students to be adaptable, future-oriented, and capable of making meaningful contributions in a dynamic world. However, innovation should not be developed solely at the classroom level. For schools and districts, a culture of innovation must be fostered within the entire educational organization. This means creating a synergy in all the spaces students enter, one that embraces experimentation, supports risk-taking, and values continuous improvement. For students to become innovators, educators must lead themselves to be innovative first. District leaders must make it a priority to provide educators with more time for professional development (PD) that includes learning, practicing, and reflecting on how best to implement innovative experiences in their classrooms. Leaders can start small by setting aside a certain amount of their budget specifically for innovative teaching and learning practices and tying it to district or state initiatives. Going back to Chapter 2, remember that all stakeholders want students to be successful. Innovative thinking may appear to be an approach that is "desirable but not essential," but it is so much more. It is the key to self-motivated students who perform well on traditional assessments *and* lead with new ideas, solutions, and possibilities.

Building the Foundation

Fostering and nurturing innovative thinking in schools is crucial, not just for the students but for educators as well. A creative mindset needs to be embraced by all, even when creativity levels are vastly different. So how do we ensure innovative thinking is part of the planning process for lessons and activities? Three approaches to support the implementation of innovative thinking are divergent thinking, convergent thinking, and lateral thinking. Each serves a unique purpose in the learning process, enhancing future-ready skills and problem solving. Let's take a closer look.

- **Divergent thinking:** This way of thinking encourages exploration of multiple solutions, ideas, or perspectives when challenged with a problem or task (Cropley, 2016). The approach is open-ended. It starts with a driving question and gives students the ability to explore a wide variety of ideas and push the envelope further than a typical classroom assignment. Divergent thinking supports learners who may struggle with creativity and critical thinking, particularly in subjects like art, creative writing, and classes that lean on project-based learning. When you design activities that encourage brainstorming, imagination, and free expression, students are better able to unlock their creative potential and develop a sense of intellectual curiosity.

    Example: A teacher provides an open-ended question (design a multimedia device) that requires students to create multiple ideations to fit the given criteria.

- **Convergent thinking:** This approach helps students choose the most effective solution from the options created during the divergent thinking step (Ramachandran, 2012). Convergent thinking is more structured and analytical. This process develops critical thinking and problem-solving skills by analyzing information, evaluating each potential solution, and concluding with a single approach. In the classroom, you can implement convergent thinking via debates, complex problems, and theoretical knowledge in real-world situations. This helps students balance creativity with practicality.

Example: An educator gives students a project and offers a list of ways to successfully complete the project. Students assess the list and evaluate which option is best suited for them and provide evidence.

- **Lateral thinking:** This type of thinking reinforces innovation by thinking creatively and solving challenging problems from extreme, unexpected angles. Lateral thinking breaks the mold of traditional patterns and explores potential alternatives that may not have been immediately obvious. This approach is highly beneficial in STEM (Science, Technology, Engineering, and Mathematics) subjects, requiring innovation and adaptability. The power of lateral thinking cultivates a mindset that values curiosity, flexibility, and confidence to take risks. Therefore, students learn to challenge problems with an open mind, to question existing assumptions about previous knowledge, and to develop ways to innovate and break away from non-linear pathways.

Example: Students receive the assignment to create a timeline of major events, but instead of a standard chronological layout, they are asked to present the timeline in a unique and creative way, like a comic strip or a social media feed. This approach encourages students to be creative about how they communicate historical events while making connections between past and modern storytelling techniques.

Using these three approaches, students and educators have a comprehensive foundation for innovative thinking that supports students as they continue striving toward creativity and analytical thinking.

Promoting Idea Generation and Adaptability

Ideally, classrooms all over the world are cultivating innovation and ideation with students. When *students* take the lead creating new ideas, concepts, and solutions, they learn the ability to adjust to new conditions and challenges. Idea generation pushes student thinking beyond what's expected in a typical classroom. This, in turn, leads to engaging and stimulating lessons that address the diversity of student needs in a classroom, which results in unique solutions and outcomes for each learner.

Adaptability helps students and teachers embrace change and think creatively when faced with new challenges, while also fostering resilience to overcome setbacks and persist through difficulties. By creating a classroom culture where failure is not viewed as a negative outcome but instead an essential part of learning, educators can help students build confidence in their ability to grow.

For example, consider a STEM class tasked with building a weight-bearing bridge using only popsicle sticks and glue. The initial attempts would often result in bridges collapsing under even the smallest of loads. Rather than seeing these as failures, students are encouraged to analyze what went wrong, ideate solutions, and rebuild. With each iteration, they refine their designs and discover innovative ways to make their structures stronger. By the end of the project, students begin to recognize how much they have learned from their failures and how that knowledge leads to celebrations of their success.

This hands-on example mirrors the mindset of design thinking, where failure is not an end result, but a method of gaining valuable information; it is a lesson that can launch an idea forward. When consistently applied, this approach can diminish the fear of failure and empower students to approach challenges with confidence and creativity.

Strategies for Idea Generation and Adaptability

Intelligence and creativity can be developed, but both need to be practiced over and over. Effort and a positive attitude can help, but students need time and repetition to become confident in their ability to hold and process knowledge, as well as find creative ways to show they have mastered skills or content. When students assess their own learning experiences and adapt how and when they are receiving information, they learn that there is more room for adjustment and their learning path is not set in stone. Understanding this truth helps students to take calculated risks, try new things, and adjust their mindset toward their learning overall. Their confidence and skill set increases with each adjustment, which sets them up for an easier transition into real-world scenarios.

Here are a few easy strategies that support idea generation and adaptability with students:

▶▶▶ **Brainstorming sessions:** Provide students with a safe space to share ideas freely without the concern of judgment or pushback from their peers (Unin & Bering, 2016). Brainstorming supports creative growth and gives students opportunities to express thoughts in a safe, collaborative environment, leading to greater confidence. One way to easily practice this process is to implement Socratic Seminars (Facing History & Ourselves, 2020) and give students the chance to lead the discussion. To better facilitate sessions, you should clearly set and state norms (amount of prep time, referring to research or textbooks when speaking, hand raising, time to speak, interruptions) and start with a few driving questions to guide the discussion.

▷ *ISTE Student Standards: Empowered Learner 1.1.a; Global Collaborator 1.7.c,1.7.d. ISTE Educator Standards: Collaborator 2.4.b; Facilitator 2.6.a*

▷ *TLPs: Nuture: Ensure Equity; Guide: Spark Curiosity*

▷ *AIM Framework: Academic Excellence, Interpersonal Skills, Mastery of Self*

▶▶▶ **Inquiry-based learning:** Give students an open-ended question that can result in various solutions. This strategy nurtures curiosity and a deeper understanding of the process of analyzing pros and cons of a particular solution. This leads students to see that even if they have a favorite or more desirable solution, it might not be the best approach for that given problem and the variables presented (Friesen & Scott, 2013).

▷ *ISTE Student Standards: Knowledge Constructor 1.3.d; Innovative Designer 1.4.d; Global Collaborator 1.7.c, 1.7.d. ISTE Educator Standard: Facilitator 2.6.a*

▷ *TLPs: Nurture: Connect Learning to the Learner, Ensure Equity; Guide: Spark Curiosity, Develop Expertise; Empower: Prioritize Authentic Experiences*

▷ *AIM Framework: Academic Excellence, Mastery of Self*

▶▶▶ **Group work:** Collaboration is vital to idea generation because students bring diverse perspectives to a project when working together. In turn, this brings forward a variety of ideas that the group can mold into a stronger and more relevant solution (McMahon et al., 2016).

▷ *ISTE Student Standards: Knowledge Constructor 1.3.d; Innovative Designer 1.4.d; Global Collaborator 1.7.c,1.7.d. ISTE Educator Standards: Learner 2.1.c; Leader 2.2.b; Collaborator 2.4.b*

▷ *TLPs: Nurture: Connect Learning to the Learner; Guide: Spark Curiosity, Empower: Ignite Agency*

▷ *AIM Framework: Academic Excellence, Interpersonal Skills, Mastery of Self*

Leverage Technologies for Idea Generation

Implementing technologies can elevate the creative process by giving students new mediums to express their ideas, but looking for the right tool for the right job is just as important. Here are some of the key characteristics and features you (and your tools) will need for some common activities:

- **Project management:** The importance of a good project management tool lies in its ability to be intuitive, adaptable, and aligned with your objectives. It should offer functionalities like organization, priority setting, progress tracking, and real-time collaboration and communication. Additionally, the tool must be scalable to manage individual, group, or class-wide projects, ensuring it meets diverse classroom needs.

- **File management:** An effective online file management system should provide secure, organized locations for storing, managing, and sharing files and folders. It should also enable multiple users to access, edit, and contribute to files in real time, fostering collaboration and streamlining workflows.

- **Coding:** Learning to code requires an interactive, hands-on approach and project-based development, regardless of the programming language. The application should offer a clear progression, starting with foundational concepts and gradually introducing more complex topics, helping students build their skills systematically and with confidence.

- **Collaborative design:** Collaborative design tools should combine intuitive usability with features like a drag-and-drop interface and real-time collaboration. These tools should empower students to explore their creativity and bring ideas to life, encouraging both individual expression and teamwork.

To discover high-quality tools to use in your classroom, visit Common Sense Education (scan the chapter's QR code for a link). Providing trusted reviews, curated recommendations, and insights on a wide range of educational tools, this resource is helpful to find the right tools to enhance learning and foster creativity in your students.

Creativity's Role in Student Learning

For students, creativity is an expression of their thoughts, ideas, and understanding. When a student is asked to showcase what they know creatively, they are not just creating a colorful presentation. Instead, they are demonstrating how they think, perceive, and interpret the world in relation to what they have learned.

Creativity allows students to express their ideas and knowledge in ways that echo their unique interests—music, art, digital media, writing, or something else entirely. Giving students options about how they share their learning beyond the typical book report, speech, or poster presentation is a start to accommodating students and embracing the idea that all learners are leaders. An idea you could use in your classroom that may elevate creativity for the entire class is a Living Museum project in which each student or group of students embodies a historical figure or a specific role (protester, journalist, or policymaker) from a time like the Civil Rights Movement, Ancient Civilization, or the Industrial Revolution. During a class event, students present their perspectives through costumes, props, or multimedia, making history come to life while showcasing their understanding in a highly personal and creative way. To really get students thinking creatively and critically, you could adapt this idea and have students create mock social media profiles, posts, or short videos from the perspectives of the historical figure and expand that to have them working in groups of two or more enabling their historical figures to "converse" together. Engaging in this type of project not only deepens engagement but also gives students an opportunity to explore the material through a unique lens and potential ways to express themselves in their learning.

▶ *ISTE Student Standards: Knowledge Constructor 1.3.a, 1.3.c; Creative Communicator 1.6.a, 1.6.b, 1.6.d; Global Collaborator 1.7.c. ISTE Educator Standards: Learner 2.1.c; Leader 2.2.b; Collaborator 2.4.b; Designer 2.5.a, 2.5.b, 2.5.c; Facilitator 2.6.a, 2.6.d*

▶ *TLPs: Nurture: Connect Learning to the Learner, Ensure Equity; Guide: Spark Curiosity, Develop Expertise; Empower: Prioritize Authentic Experiences, Ignite Agency*

▶ *AIM Framework: Academic Excellence, Interpersonal Skills, Mastery of Self*

Creative expression opens the ability for students to explore different ways of communicating, engaging with the content on a more personal level and discovering connections between their passions, academia, and the world around them. When creative work is valued and recognized, it boosts students' self-esteem and encourages them to take on new and potentially difficult challenges because they find learning more natural and enjoyable, leading to greater motivation and a sense of self-worth. Furthermore, the creative process requires experimentation, trial and error, and learning from mistakes, helping students understand that challenges are growth opportunities rather than setbacks or barriers.

Creativity is not just an addition to the learning process. It should be at the top of your priority list because it sparks thinking and dynamically expands students' abilities to make confident decisions in classrooms and beyond.

Transitioning to Authentic Assessment

We have established that innovative thinking, creativity, and idea generation can fundamentally transform a student's learning, but how do you evolve from assessing students based on the number of correct test answers to a more open, authentic response that can be presented in various ways? How can there possibly be enough time to authentically assess students *and* do everything else being asked of teachers? We're not promising the task is easy or without obstacles, but small changes with instruction, student collaboration, and assessment can transform the classroom experience for students and teachers in a big way over time.

One place to start is by rethinking assessment objectives and redesigning them to be open-ended with multiple correct answers instead of leaning solely on standardized or multiple-choice exams. Students need to practice learning information, re-learning as often as needed, and then confidently be able to illustrate and speak to that learning without the assistance of a possible answers list and a lucky guess. Project-based learning (PBL) is one way to incorporate this process, but it's also a lofty goal when just starting to embrace the mindset of authentic assessment. During PBL, students participate in long-term projects that require research, design, and implementation of solutions. PBL promotes deeper learning experiences, showcases innovative thinking and performance-based assessment (presentations, portfolios, simulations), and requires students to demonstrate the validity of their learning. Project-based learning and performance-based assessments both take a great deal of planning, so here are a few small ways to begin practicing this approach with students (Ruman, 2024):

▶▶▶ **Visual storytelling:** Ask students to tell a story about something they learned in class using visual storytelling like a comic strip or storyboard. You can evaluate a student's creativity, narrative structure, and artistic techniques from there and any other objectives you find helpful.

▶ *ISTE Student Standards: Innovative Designer 1.4.a, 1.4.b; Creative Communicator 1.6.c, 1.6.d. ISTE Educator Standards: Designer 2.5.a, 2.5.b, 2.5.c; Facilitator 2.6.a*

▶ *TLPs: Nurture: Connect Learning to the Learner, Ensure Equity; Guide: Develop Expertise; Empower: Prioritize Authentic Experiences*

▶ *AIM Framework: Academic Excellence, Interpersonal Skills, Mastery of Self*

▶▶▶ **Build a simple machine:** Task students to design and create a simple machine (lever, pulley system), using everyday materials (paper, straws, string). Students can then explain how it works and demonstrate its functionality via any format the student prefers including presentation, creating a video, recording an audio explanation, or some mix of approaches. This assignment introduces mechanical principles, creativity in design, and communication skills.

▶ *ISTE Student Standards: Innovative Designer 1.4.a, 1.4.b, 1.4.c; Global Collaborator 1.7.c. ISTE Educator Standards: Collaborator 2.4.b; Designer 2.5.a, 2.5.b, 2.5.c*

▶ *TLPs: Nurture: Connect Learning to the Learner; Guide: Develop Expertise; Empower: Prioritize Authentic Experiences*

▶ *AIM Framework: Academic Excellence, Interpersonal Skills*

▶▶▶ **Book trailer:** Ask students to create a short video trailer for a book or novel that they have read. The trailer can explain the plot, introduce the characters, and present the theme without any spoilers. Allowing students to include multimedia solutions supports comprehension, creativity, and presentation skills.

▶ *ISTE Student Standards: Innovative Designer 1.4.a, 1.4.b, 1.4.c. ISTE Educator Standards: Leader 2.2.b; Designer 2.5.a, 2.5.b, 2.5.c; Facilitator 2.6.a, 2.6.b*

▶ *TLPs: Guide: Spark Curiosity, Develop Expertise; Empower: Prioritize Authentic Experiences*

▶ *AIM Framework: Academic Excellence, Interpersonal Skills, Mastery of Self*

▶▶▶ **Eco-friendly product proposal:** Students work in groups to create a proposal for an eco-friendly product that addresses an environmental problem, such as reducing food waste or conserving water. Each group member contributes a design idea, and collectively the group votes on the most compelling design to refine. Alternatively, the entire class could review all proposals and vote on the most compelling design to move forward with. The selected proposal should detail the environmental issue being addressed, explain the potential environmental impact of the solution, and showcase innovative thinking in both design and implementation. This assessment requires students to demonstrate an understanding of environmental issues and scientific concepts while enhancing creativity, teamwork, and persuasive communication skills during their presentation.

- *ISTE Student Standards: Empowered Learner 1.1.a; Innovative Designer 1.4.a, 1.4.b, 1.4.c, 1.4.d; Creative Commuicator 1.6.c; Global Collaborator 1.7.c, 1.7.d. ISTE Educator Standards: Learner 2.1.c; Designer 2.5.a*

- *TLPs: Nurture: Connect Learning to the Learner; Guide: Spark Curiosity, Develop Expertise; Empower: Prioritize Authentic Experiences*

- *AIM Framework: Academic Excellence, Interpersonal Skills, Mastery of Self*

▶▶▶ **Podcasting:** Students may work individually creating short audio snippets of their learning to become accustomed to the podcast creation process. Utilizing student-approved technologies that include audio/video features like familiar social applications are a great way to introduce podcasting to students and get them comfortable hearing their own voice. To challenge students a bit more, have them work in small groups on separate projects or together to contribute to a larger production. As students begin setting goals (AIM: Mastery of Self) and using the design-thinking process (AIM: Academic Excellence, Interpersonal Skills), you will see in an organic and authentic way whether students have learned academic content and are able to successfully complete a project over a grading period or several grading periods. To support student-led podcasting in your classroom, we have included a planning template, example script, and grading rubric in the QR code–linked resources.

- *ISTE Student Standards: Creative Communicator 1.6.a, 1.6.b, 1.6.c, 1.6.d; Global Collaborator 1.7.c. ISTE Educator Standards: Leader 2.2.b; Collaborator 2.4.b; Designer 2.5.a, 2.5.b, 2.5.c; Facilitator 2.6.a, 2.6.b*

- *TLPs: Nurture: Ensure Equity; Guide: Spark Curiosity, Develop Expertise; Empower: Prioritize Authentic Experiences, Ignite Agency*

- *AIM Framework: Academic Excellence, Interpersonal Skills, Mastery of Self*

Throughout the year, it is vital to check in with students to see how they are performing and to ensure they consume, process, and understand the material, while consistently maintaining the pace of the class. This can be done with a *formative assessment*, a quick method that shows each student's mastery of small pieces of information at a time. This approach helps you and your students assess high performance or if a student may need intervention or supplemental support to confidently move on to the next portion of learning. Right now, the most common approach to formative assessment is quizzes or brief check-ins that review what has just been taught in the classroom. Other options that require a minimum of your time are observation of student engagement with collaborative projects and learning journals, in which students can reflect daily or weekly on what they have learned. You could also allow students to self-assess their work or learning with a two- or three-item checklist. At the end of a lesson, you could ask students to write down (digitally or physically) one thing they have learned and one question they still have. Checking these "exit tickets" is another way to see if the objectives are being met (Dyer, 2024). Which one is "best"? The answer depends on several factors. Consider the end goal of your formative assessment activity, and choose the most appropriate option for the time frame, content, and tools available.

Whichever method you choose, include the student and give them a voice in their assessment process so they understand how they are being evaluated, which criteria are required, and how feedback and self-reflection will be addressed. This could be as thorough as a student-led conference or as simple as allowing students the chance to submit their ideas on criteria or how they present their learning (graphic, presentation, drawing, animation, written report, video, audio podcast). This allows students time to reflect on their learning and empowers them to think more critically and creatively about their work. By supporting students with continuous and constructive feedback, educators can guide students in improving and enhancing their ideas. This process helps students gain a growth mindset, in which assessment is used for learning rather than completion-only work or tests. With the inclusion of innovative thinking in the assessment process, you can create richer, more authentic evaluations of each student. Evolving to authentic assessment is not about just changing the tools that you use to measure learning, but also about adopting a more holistic approach that focuses on value and strengthening a student's abilities.

Innovation Generates Authentic Assessment

The transition to authentic assessment is not a simple switch; however, innovative thinking is a pivotal step toward capturing a student's genuine understanding and abilities. A one-size-fits-all approach will not work in education because it does not meet all students' needs. Innovative thinking meets students where they are with a more personalized and tailored experience. Measuring a student's performance should be about how they think and how they solve problems, not just their score on an exam or their final grade on a report card. All stakeholders must embrace a shift in mindset and lead by example with creativity, experimentation, and diverse instructional strategies to effectively implement authentic assessment. Aiming to explore, discover, and learn together, the collaboration between teachers and students can become a grounding force for authentic assessment and innovative thinking. As a result, teachers as well as students will inspire others to adopt a similar approach toward teaching and learning.

tinyurl.com/
TodaysLearners

Scan the QR code to access resources associated with this chapter.

CHAPTER 7

Digital Portfolios:
The Future of CVs

Standards and Principles Addressed

The content of this chapter aligns with the following standards, indicators, and principles:

ISTE Student Standards

Empowered Learner (1.1.a, 1.1.c)

Digital Citizen (1.2.a, 1.2.b, 1.2.c, 1.2.d)

Knowledge Constructor (1.3.a, 1.3.b, 1.3.c, 1.3.d)

ISTE Educator Standards

Learner (2.1.a, 2.1.c)

Leader (2.2.a, 2.2.b, 2.2.c)

Citizen (2.3.a, 2.3.b, 2.3.c, 2.3.d)

Collaborator (2.4.b, 2.4.c, 2.4.d)

Designer (2.5.a, 2.5.b, 2.5.c)

Facilitator (2.6.a, 2.6.b, 2.6.c, 2.6.d)

Analyst (2.7.a, 2.7.b)

Transformational Learning Principles

Nurture: Connect Learning to Learner, Ensure Equity

Guide: Spark Curiosity, Develop Expertise, Evaluate Reflection

Empower: Prioritize Authentic Experiences, Ignite Agency

The Portfolio Is Proof

Evidence of learning is the most powerful way to confirm whether someone has truly mastered a skill or specific knowledge, and a learning portfolio is one way to collect that evidence. Anyone can say they possess a particular skill, have key knowledge to meet measurable goals, or possess the ability to create a specific deliverable, but to *show* evidence of skills, goals met, and creative designs is more powerful than any words on a resume.

One day in 2018 while Tisha was driving this idea home to students, a colleague happened to be fixing a tech issue in the classroom and chimed in, "The portfolio is proof." From that day forward, Tisha's classroom ran on the idea that a resume is a promise of what we can do, and the portfolio is proof. Those students (some of whom you have heard from in previous chapters) held tightly to that concept and never looked back.

Portfolio Evolution

So, what exactly is a learning portfolio? To best answer this, let's review what a learning portfolio was in the 1990s. While the world was grasping onto the idea of the World Wide Web, learning portfolios were a physical collection of a student's work over time. Tisha remembers compiling her undergrad work in a leather binder with a physical print copy of each writing assignment, project, award, certificate, reflection, and report card, tucked neatly into a sheet protector. Additionally, she included her resume, cover letter, references, teaching certificate, classroom management plan, and example lesson plans because her goal was to land a teaching job with her "evidence briefcase." Her learning portfolio was the outcome and final step for her undergraduate degree and teacher-driven with little room for student autonomy. This tangible curation of her performance made it easy for potential employers to review real-life examples of her work while she shared stories of her experiences with her bachelor's studies and years of student teaching. It is no surprise that her interviews went well and gave her confidence in her teaching abilities far beyond the grades included on her transcript.

As it was for Tisha, a *learning portfolio* for today's students is a comprehensive snapshot of a student's growth and development across a single subject of study or across multiple disciplines. This snapshot becomes a tool for student reflection encouraging students to think through their learning process, and then the portfolio becomes a showcase presentation to share with parents and peers or to be submitted for special programs, internships, or scholarships. Additionally, portfolios can be used by teachers to better assess how students are meeting learning standards and objectives over time. The difference between Tisha's portfolios and those of today's students is mostly related to their format.

As the Web continued to transform the world around us and personal computers became a popular household item, this also marked a pivotal point in the evolution of educational technology. Tisha's experience as a learner and then a teacher during this time gave her insight into the progress of a learning portfolio, while simultaneously new digital tools and learning management platforms entered classrooms across the world. Learning portfolios were no longer limited to leather binders and paper contents; they were reimagined to include digital evidence. Rather than relying on printouts of written reflections, portfolios could contain videos of learners personally sharing reflections. (Note: From this point forward, we will use the terms *portfolio*, *digital portfolio*, *learning portfolio*, and *digital learning portfolio* interchangeably. Our emphasis will be on learning, reflection, and showcasing regardless of format.)

Think of a digital portfolio as a student-created museum or gallery where each section and artifact (visual, interactive multimedia) show a unique point in a student's learning journey. Browsing the portfolio, you can easily see their skills, achievements, creativity, and growth. There are a multitude of choices for students to create a digital portfolio, but each displayed piece in the museum might showcase the student's best and most prized work *and* might show their process of overcoming a struggle and including the lessons they learned along the way. They transform from a student into a museum curator, artist, historian, storyteller, and visitor. They get to lead others into the story of themselves and craft the details to tell the world what they know and what they are capable of.

Benefits of Portfolios

Tisha's students' experience with portfolios transformed their classroom experiences and fostered a love for learning and reflection. They began asking each other opinions on how best to showcase their content, accepted invitations to share their experiences with global audiences as guests on webinars and virtual conferences, and came to realize their portfolio creations did not have to stop after they left her classroom or high school. Seeing students learn, expand, and apply new and existing skills to fully complete the learning cycle to the reflection stage was truly the highlight of Tisha's teaching career. Most often, teachers never get to see the full scope and impact of a student's learning in a single year.

Students quickly realized that curating artifacts to show evidence of learning gave them a true picture of their growth in a certain subject or skill, something their report cards had never been able to show. Curating a learning portfolio also gave them ownership of their decision-making (AIM), and even more important, it gave them a head start when it came to college and job applications.

Grades and assessments are necessary and required, but they provide only a small part of the complete picture of the learning cycle. How often do we teachers guide students to create a learning timeline that shows their efforts, adaptability, skills, and knowledge inside *and* outside of the classroom? We know that students are much more than a test score. A digital learning portfolio might include achievements with grades, but it also opens the door for creativity and storytelling showcasing who students are academically *and* personally. Digital learning portfolios offer evidence of all the AIM Framework skills (Chapter 2) combined in a visual format that empowers students to lead and adjust their learning for future goals (ISTE Student Standards 1.1.a, 1.1.c; TLP Empower). For example, students apply their knowledge of digital tools to curate and creatively express their learning (Academic Excellence) and learn how to effectively communicate their reasoning for making certain choices with which platform they are using to showcase their work or create the visual aspects of their overall portfolio presentation (Interpersonal Skills). Making decisions on which individual assignments, creative content, or collaborative projects to include in a learning portfolio refines confidence and self-reliance and gives a sense of accomplishment with achieving smaller tasks that eventually lead to a larger completed goal (Master of Self). Curating the "best of" their work naturally requires reflection and critical thinking and creates a path for students to move forward. A student's portfolio precedes their presence and becomes a living testament to what they know, how they work, and what is possible. The implementation of digital portfolios in your classroom will help you see a much larger scope of progress instead of the small snapshot in time that an assessment gives.

As emerging technologies change the landscape of learning, digital portfolios will continue to evolve. With the onset of Web3 (which utilizes artificial intelligence), each of us might have a digital wallet with a unique passkey that stores our most valuable information. Like a digital safety deposit box, you could store insurance cards, passport details, boarding passes, and hotel reservations, as well as your high school transcripts, college degrees, and any certificates of learning you earn.

Digital Identity as a Portfolio

A *digital portfolio* is a collection of work, skills, or experiences that are curated in a single digital space accessible to the public typically, but also possibly unlisted or private depending on the purpose and intended audience. Whether you realize it or not, you've probably had experience creating one already. How? Your social media accounts—and your students are likely doing the same.

With the emergence of social media in the mid-2000s, students began using their "free" computer time to visit sites like Facebook, MySpace, and Xanga. Tisha can remember watching social media slowly take over students' attention and wondering what it was about those sites that captivated them so much. As many generations do, adults were quick to restrict or ban use of these sites in their classrooms without the support of the filters and today's digital safety nets.

Tisha, however, became curious. This new technology was not going away, and she anticipated early on that it could potentially impact education and learning in a massive way. She immediately joined each social media site to better understand the end-user experience and started ideating ways to leverage this technology for teaching and learning. She then began connecting the experiences of social media to the classroom: Students wanted to connect with each other in a collaborative and engaging way; they could do this on a social media platform. Students wanted to be creative and design in a way that expressed their individuality; they could do this with social media. The questions Tisha asked then are the same as we're asking today: If social media offers something our classrooms are not, how can we change that? How can educators take the good parts of social media and combine them with the meaningful aspects of the classroom to change the way students are learning and engaging?

As technology is constantly evolving and platforms are updating the way users can connect, share, and engage with the world, students generally do not see a problem with social media. In fact, they believe it gives them great benefits including making new friends, promoting creativity, and learning about other cultures and people (Prothero, 2024). Tisha and Rick would add that social media brings about an environment of microlearning that has impacted the way we all engage with information, giving way to a network of learning we have not had before. Additionally, social media is giving students a real-world example of how creativity, curation, collaboration, and critical thinking can be applied for good. In the social media and online world, students are creators, curators, and collaborators. Can we say the same for students in our classrooms?

Social post commenting allows opportunities for giving and receiving positive feedback and communicating with others. Students who are using social media or have had opportunities to create mock accounts learn how to critically think through the validity of information shared and learn how posting, commenting, and liking posts create a narrative or a "story" without saying much at all. They are essentially learning digital citizenship and information literacy skills on their own, often without our guidance. Educators may think of these skills as important for an awareness week or a particular unit of learning only, but students are faced with learning these skills on a minute-by-minute basis.

We all have created "micro digital portfolios" with our social media accounts, curating the best photos, thoughts, ideas, videos, and articles. Dare we say that each social media account is a living resume or digital portfolio and is a testament to who we are, what we do, and what we know? How do we leverage what students know about social spaces, curation, and creativity, and then help them apply that knowledge to a learning portfolio that provides evidence of growth over time, a CV (curriculum vitae) or resume to show evidence of work experiences, and prepare them to share and take ownership of it all *even after they leave our classrooms?*

Why Digital Portfolios

Scaling a digital learning portfolio project for hundreds of middle school or high school students may seem like a mountain of an activity—but don't let that deter you. Starting small with the concept of a learning portfolio is key. As with any goal, working little by little consistently over time will always catapult you forward. Scope out the end learning goal, and then work backwards. Planning checkpoints along the way helps break the project up into smaller chunks of learning and feedback and can make implementing learning portfolios less daunting.

Jace, a high school freshman who attends a school in Grapevine-Colleyville ISD, shared that his classes incorporate the idea of a digital portfolio that counts as 35% of the student's overall grade. Throughout each grading period, students are asked to complete "portfolio assignments" that include a specific grading rubric to teach students how to show their learning effectively and includes specific feedback (AIM: Interpersonal Skills) portions with opportunities to improve their final product (AIM: Master of Self). Over the course of the year, each portfolio activity measures what students know with an exam or quiz (AIM: Academic Excellence) but *also* includes an authentic assessment of the individual student.

While it can be easy to dismiss the implementation of portfolios because it seems overwhelming due to time and testing restraints, we argue the benefits of student digital portfolios outweigh any of the reasons we could come up with for *not* doing them. For example, a 2022 study assessed two groups of students taking a writing course, and the group that *did* create portfolios saw improvement in writing performance, organization, and focus (Zaabalawi & Zaabalawi, 2024).

In addition, digital learning portfolios support student success beyond the classroom. The following sections delve deeper into how.

Tracking Progress with Feedback

The most common methods of tracking student progress—traditional grades, assignments, and testing—often lack a follow-through component of feedback or reflection. The main goal of a portfolio, however, is to track learning progress with a more holistic and authentic approach. Digital portfolios enable teachers and students to see learning over time, intervene if necessary, and address any concerns that may arise. Some schools are required to implement portfolios to track learning with the aim to validate grant monies received for specific academic programs. Many schools may pick a specific digital tool to help them achieve this, but it is important to remember that simplicity is sometimes more effective than a robust process or tool.

The goal is for students to be able to *see* their improvement in a certain area of learning: writing, reading, creativity, math application, science hypothesis, self-advocacy, public speaking, or elsewhere. Strategic implementation of realistic, task-based checkpoints that make sense for your students and classroom is one of the best ways to consistently track progress and keep everyone on pace.

Fostering Learner Agency and Ownership

Learning guides or rubrics can direct and assist students with the overall structure of a portfolio's organization and design, as well as encourage them to practice asking themselves questions and making decisions about their own project in ways that supports their unique experiences and ideas. Guiding students through this process rather than giving them an exact blueprint places teachers in a true facilitating role and the student in the role of a leader. A single-point grading rubric is an easy solution. If you're unfamiliar with utilizing a rubric, a little research will yield many examples for review.

Tisha changed from using a traditional rubric to a single-point rubric for a few reasons. She felt that a traditional rubric limited students from reaching their full potential because it directly outlined the minimum requirements for a passing grade. The single-point rubric gave students a simple target for each assignment and project and left ample room for growth and feedback. FIGURE 7.1 offers a snapshot of Tisha's rubric, showing the bull's-eye students might want to aim for as they begin creating their portfolio and choosing which of their best artifacts to include. (Scan the QR code at the end of the chapter to download the full rubric.)

Concerns	Criteria	Advanced
	Purpose: Appropriate for audience, organized for easy navigation, well-thought out categories/headings	
	Content: 10-20 items showcasing your learning, skills, achievements, creativity, growth, reflections	
	Design: Use of the 4 design principles: Contrast, Repetition, Alignment, Proximity are evident	

Digital Portfolio Rubric for _____   Rate Your Own Portfolio _____

Overall Feedback & Reflections:

FIGURE 7.1
Tisha's single-point grading rubric

It is important to outline *choices* to prompt students but not to confine them to a rigid structure. This may feel uncomfortable, as it did for Tisha in the beginning, but remember, there is *a* way, not *the* way. If your students arrive successfully at the end learning goal of the portfolio, *how* they get there should be up to them. With this type of support, a portfolio project becomes an opportunity for learners to practice decision-making skills, choosing which work they deem as their best, comparing the pros and cons of district-approved applications, deciding which tool best assists with organization, structure, and design. When students have choices within the guidelines of the teacher and the learning objectives, the portfolio individualizes and personalizes learning in ways that typical assessments cannot.

When created with a larger audience in mind (whole class, school, parents, school board, community, colleges, employers), portfolios give students confidence, ownership, and a real-world audience outside of their typical classroom. By cultivating this mindset, portfolios elevate the classroom from a place where assignments are "just for a grade" into a place of curiosity and discovery where students fully come to understand how their curated work is a "digital briefcase," growing and transforming along with them.

Facilitating Collaboration

Student collaboration is one way to teach students the art of peer-to-peer feedback. Digital learning portfolios are a perfect way to incorporate this into the entire school year by correlating grading checkpoints with previous peer-to-peer feedback. Portfolios give students a chance to really see their peers' strengths and individuality, as well as their own. For maybe the first time in their learning journey, they are given a chance (with teacher guidance) to learn *how* to offer thoughtful feedback and *receive* suggestions without taking it as a personal attack on their performance. Moments of collaboration can be short with little consumption of time. Using a basic learning management system's capability of commenting and replying, students can link their portfolio and ask for feedback from peers (Chapter 8 offers additional ideas to implement with students). Another idea might be to use a whole-class digital whiteboard, so students can drop their portfolio link onto the board and quickly visit another student's link for a quick review and indicate it's been reviewed and seen with a thumbs up, like, heart, or other available feature.

Tisha and her students loved using video or audio to collaborate and execute peer-to-peer feedback. Getting students comfortable with this method did not happen overnight, though. Tisha's classroom culture started out with the expectation that students would get comfortable speaking and recording—at first with themselves as the only audience, and later with each other. The technologies you choose to utilize and when you introduce them to students are completely up to you, but using a tool or platform students are already comfortable with can help them focus on the process of collaboration and feedback. Allowing time for students to discuss and communicate with each other about their portfolio reinforces a real-world setting of teamwork and project management.

Beginning with Reflection

The learning process consists of planning, teaching and learning, assessment, analyzing, adapting, and reflecting. For time-starved teachers, completing this process can be difficult. So how can we each build it into the other phases we focus on the most? With a portfolio, students *begin* by reflecting on what they have learned, where they have improved, and where they want to go next in their learning. To begin a lesson or project with reflection detours the traditional learning process through valuable critical thinking. Students are asked to think through their work performance, writing samples, designs, or multimedia projects and ask questions of themselves and others:

- Is this my best work?
- Am I comfortable sharing this with an audience other than my teacher or classmates?
- Which pieces of work show my progress best?
- Is this work sample something I can take with me to the next class, college, or job?
- How can I improve and create better examples of my abilities?
- What should I change or edit?
- Which samples or designs portray me and my skills best?

When students show their learning within a portfolio, they become accustomed to the consistent feedback and reflection and will naturally improve this over time.

Practicing Real-World Skills

Our current students are digital natives, but this does not exclude them from needing technology skills, support, and modeling. Portfolio projects require a certain level of problem-solving and decision-making. Implementing digital learning portfolios inside of a classroom or school curriculum gives students a low-stakes environment to practice and refine technology skills, enabling them to prepare for using similar skills in future learning and work environments. Our end goal is for our students to be learners today who develop a motivation to learn, successfully apply knowledge, and become leaders tomorrow.

Shaping Personal Brands and Stories

When we read *personal brand*, we tend to immediately think of social media influencers who have a following and have earned trust with their followers by sharing their expertise in fitness, fashion, or entertainment. Personal branding is not just meant for those who publicly share or stay "on trend." Branding is important for us all to consider—whether we have zero followers or one million. It shows the intention to stay up to date in our preferred industry and highlights unique skills, talents, and experiences. Additionally, personal branding helps give us an identity of resiliency and awareness, which could set us apart from others when applying for opportunities that attract many applicants.

Building a positive presence online is an increasingly important skill as technologies continue to transform and shape into something new. As mentioned before, social influence and technological literacy are listed as one of the top skills we all need to have before 2025 (Masterson, 2023). Equally important and essentially going hand-in-hand with personal branding are digital citizenship and digital literacy skills. The ability to confidently share and engage with others online positively or spotting inconsistencies with information online is a lifelong skill we cannot afford to ignore. Learning these skills and practicing them over and over ensures that we are being mindful with our personal brand and message.

Many educators are looking to organizations like ISTE to help guide students with digital citizenship competencies throughout the year, but in Tisha's experience, many schools address digital citizenship only one week per the year: Digital Citizenship Week. Created in 2012 by Common Sense Media, Digital Citizenship Week was established to raise awareness and recognize districts, schools, and teachers who were creating a culture of positive digital citizenship (Mendoza, 2022). While this awareness week has been a powerful reminder that digital citizenship is a skill needed by everyone of all ages, there are still large gaps with teaching these skills daily across all grades and classes. So how can we use what we know about personal branding to help guide our students to develop a positive self-image and share their stories to leverage opportunities for their future?

For a start, you can ask students to share words, ideas, or values that best describe themselves to get to know them better. You can take this practice a step further and have students expand the typical All About Me projects from the first week of school to create a personal brand. Task them to create their own logo with digital design tools, create a color palette of their favorite color and complementary colors, and come up with three words that best describe them by asking their friends and family, "If you could describe me, my skills, or my talents using a single word, photo, or emoji, what would it be?" From this curated list, students can then pick out the three to five they feel most align with them, begin formulating what their personal story is, and then design an image that incorporates the words, photos, and emoji along with the colors they have chosen and their logo. Now students have something much more robust than a single activity for a grade; they have something—a brand—that they can use throughout the rest of the year with their creative designs, projects, learning portfolios, or websites.

Introducing personal branding for students should be kept simple so they can continue to build upon prior knowledge, refine their stories and apply the design thinking skills we discussed in Chapter 5. For tips on branding, scan the QR code at the end of this chapter.

Implementing Portfolios with Learning

Implementing portfolios with students helps them to make sense of their experiences, find connections among ideas, and better communicate their success and struggles with certain aspects of their learning process. As Jones and Leverenz explained in the *International Journal of ePortfolio*, "Portfolios tell a story about our learning; we are not merely reflecting on our learning but actively creating a world in which we play the lead role" (2017). Documenting learning with a portfolio combines authentic assessment within the guidelines of traditional grading and helps students learn to track their progress, process obstacles and solutions and receive professional reviews, much like they will experience as they continue their education and career.

Districts, schools, and teachers are as unique as their students, so a portfolio implementation process is the opposite of a one-size-fits-all guide to follow. Each school or classroom must navigate different logistics, requirements, and obstacles. Despite this, or maybe because of it, educators must switch the focus of preliminary discussions from "here is why we cannot implement learning portfolios" to "we believe learning is important for our students and so are the opportunities to *apply* their learning so they begin succeeding *now*."

Once that mindset change is made, you can start planning and thinking about how digital portfolios might look in your district or classroom. As you read through this chapter, make notes of which practices are mostly teacher-led (purpose) and which practices are student-led (content, design). To challenge yourself a bit, consider which practices might benefit from more student input. For inspiration and some students' perspectives on this topic, we recommend listening to what Tisha's students had to say in the "Digital Portfolios (No. 4)" episode of *SWATIFY*, a podcast created by Students Who Advocate Technology (SWAT). For implementation ideas and practices Tisha found helpful when working with students, read on to the following sections.

Define a Purpose

The first step in the implementation process is to identify the purpose of the portfolio. A digital learning portfolio can serve a multitude of purposes: goal setting, authentic assessment, multimedia curation, collaborative projects, or self-directed learning. There are several ways to implement portfolios: a class-by-class basis, across a department or grade level, as a school showcase, or scaled to support a district initiative. This decision will drive who the end audience will be to review portfolios: in-class peers, grade-level peers, a single school community, parents, district leaders, school board members, or a global audience. Additionally important is to pinpoint exactly how a portfolio implementation will continue from grade to grade and school to school so that students can take their final product with them upon graduation and use it as part of their resume to apply for jobs or enter college. Ultimately, a portfolio should *very rarely* be a one-and-done assignment, but rather a project that can be applied to a future short-term or long-term goal.

Set a Project Timeline

Your next step is to establish a project timeline. When planning lessons, activities, and projects for the year, semester, or grading period, keep in mind which points or dates might be a good place to incorporate this project. One of the best ways to streamline and scale a digital portfolio is to use a student-led conference or have students keep a project journal log to keep track of their portfolio on a weekly basis as they approach each grading checkpoint. This process teaches students ownership of learning, daily self-reflection, and how to document and reflect on project progress. In addition, you can identify certain activities, assignments, or projects early on to ensure that the portfolio is being revised, refined, and reviewed consistently.

Major checkpoints at the beginning of the year, middle of the year, and end of the year allow for progress snapshots that eventually create a complete picture and story that transforms *with* the student as they grow in both learning and self. Additionally, identifying how much the portfolio will weigh in terms of a student's overall grade helps teachers, students, and parents better support the process as time goes by.

Curate Learning Standards

The next step is to curate targeted learning standards that will be met with a learning portfolio. These standards should include the required state standards along with any supplemental standards or principles (ISTE Standards, TLPs, AIM) being consistently implemented. The idea of implementing supplemental standards is not meant to be an added responsibility to teachers, but to support and reveal the *why* of the projects and activities and to transparently show students (and parents) how deeper learning can better prepare them for working with future managers or leaders. When students can quickly share what the learning goal is in a class and explain how assignments or activities assist this goal, they have taken ownership of their learning even if they have not yet mastered it.

Teachers are the artists in their classrooms. They are experts of their content and learning standards and confidently know which learning standards can be combined and met with a single project that appears to be just "an assignment for a grade." To the outside world, teachers are still standing at the front of their classrooms, lecturing, and giving timed tests. While there may still be teachers whose teaching philosophy aligns with this picture, many teachers have surpassed the initial knowledge from their pre-service education classes. Teachers have learned to lean on their team and their personal learning communities (PLC) to improve teaching practices and instructional strategies to meet required standards, incorporate supplemental standards and make learning fun, engaging and meaningful.

When using digital learning portfolios to transport students to deeper understanding and reflection of content, a shift happens that may not be evident immediately. When you pair that learning with technology, four types of learning occur (Driscoll, 2002):

- **Active learning** shifts students from learning curriculum to engaging and working with *ideas* and creates opportunities make learning visible. More and more, the education community is recognizing the benefits and power of learning by doing (AIM: Academic Excellence) instead of listening (Reigeluth & An, 2021), and digital learning portfolios lean on this skill.

- **Social learning** includes making connections between learning and broader communities and perspectives. This type of learning prompts dialogue (AIM: Interpersonal Skills) to solidify mastery and application of learning goals. Learning portfolios become social when students and teachers give and receive feedback and it becomes second nature to do so.

- **Reflective learning** allows learners to clear up any misconceptions and transfer their knowledge to problems and solutions. Additionally, reflective learning allows ample opportunity for revision without permanent consequences of "not getting it right the first time." Digital learning portfolios stand on reflective learning because there is never a true ending to the students' stories. They can go back and revise (AIM: Master of Self) as often as they see fit and may see things they have missed three reviews prior. Another connection could be made here with social media profiles as profile photos, bios, and content continuously change.

- **Real-world learning** gives students a foundational *why* and *how* of the learning and encompasses reflective, social, and active learning. It is not enough to sit in a classroom each day for hours and soak in information or learn new skills without the opportunity to put those skills into practice. In theory, you may be reading this chapter feeling very confident about learning portfolio implementation, but to execute it in a classroom with students creates a completely new experience. You may encounter challenges we haven't covered in this book—or even anticipated. Real-world learning requires self-directed learning, information analysis, and on-the-spot problem solving (AIM: Academic Excellence) that a book or exam cannot provide. As you begin implementing the ideas in this book, make a note to yourself ask if your students would say their time learning with you prepared them for future real-world situations.

Adapt Grading

Grading is a step that cannot be avoided even if students and educators want to take a more holistic approach to assessment. For this step, review the district or school grading policy and adapt your grading and checkpoints accordingly. Formative assessment for a digital portfolio project is almost more important than the final assessment because students and teachers can discuss or debate what is working and what is not and still have time to adjust any requirements or obstacles before it is too late. This method of grading also makes the final review of a portfolio much easier than you might expect. Putting time in consistently with students before the final submission is a win-win for both student *and* teacher. Checkpoints and formative assessments also ensure that every student is getting a moment in time with the teacher for feedback, reflection, praise, and encouragement. Taking time for this early on will save you time, will teach students how this process will work in their future careers or academic pursuits, and will mold them into leaders who do the same for others.

To keep students (and herself) on track, Tisha created a document that was loosely based on one she used years before as a yearbook advisor. The problem she was trying to solve then was to hold students accountable for the sections of the district-wide yearbook they were responsible for and to help them all meet deadlines set by their publishing company. When Tisha began ideating a way to show the value of her student-led classroom and their projects and activities, she went back to her experience project managing yearbooks. She needed a way to teach students how to document their daily tasks, obstacles, and wins, as well as teach them how to grade themselves on their performance before she did. The Student-Led Conference document was her solution. FIGURE 7.2 shows Tisha's original, but you can adapt it to better meet your needs; simply scan the QR code at the end of this chapter for access.

Name _____		Grade you deserve for this evaluation period: _____	
List Daily Tasks, Projects and/or Personal Goals	Date due	Date completed	Notes, Comments, Questions, Challenges, Feedback

FIGURE 7.2
Student-Led Conference document

Consider Content

Portfolio content is as individualized as your classroom décor, but the portfolio's purpose and audience will ultimately drive which content to include. STEAM or STEM students creating a digital portfolio for a parent showcase, for example, will focus on sharing projects completed over the course of the year and include their process, obstacles, and reflections. English Language Arts teachers may require a writing portfolio with argumentative and informational writing samples along with annotation examples. Art and Media student content may include creations from every unit throughout the year and the portfolios could be shared with global audiences for competitions. Language portfolios will most likely include reading, writing, listening, and speaking portions to show a student's progress so teachers can combine assessment data with a portfolio to have an accurate picture of why a student may be ahead or behind an expected learning goal. Portfolio content tells one half of a student's learning story and traditional assessment data will tell the other half. One without the other is an incomplete story, so when you're planning for content required, include as many accommodating artifacts as possible (audio, video, written text, graphics, drawings, images, presentations, and more).

Introduce Design

It is never too early to introduce design elements to students. As they continue to *show* their learning, they will naturally have an eye for what looks visually appealing and what is difficult to see or read. You can introduce a basic understanding of design elements through bell ringer tasks or daily learning warmups. Over time, students will begin to implement these aspects into their digital portfolio and expand on their own personal branding. Design elements and personal branding can be included in a grading rubric, but it is important to stress to students that these elements should come *after* the main content required. Some students can get so hyper-focused on the design elements that they lose sight of the overall end goal, so you may need to provide a bit more additional teacher guidance. Creating balance with design elements and content within a digital portfolio will provide a blueprint for students as they showcase their creativity and work samples in more professional settings. Some example concepts to include for design and personal branding include:

- Consistency (of color schemes, fonts, text sizes, styles for a professional organized feel)
- Repetition (of colors, shapes, logos to create an expected pattern or rhythm for recognition)

- Contrast (of light versus dark, big versus little, bold versus thin to make elements stand out and grab attention)
- Proximity (of related items grouped together to convey ideas or objects belong together)

Again, design and personal branding criteria will be based on past knowledge and course learning standards, so they may vary from teacher to teacher.

Promote Feedback

Tisha recommends taking a close look at the learning process (**FIGURE 7.3**) if you have not or if it has been a while.

FIGURE 7.3
The learning cycle

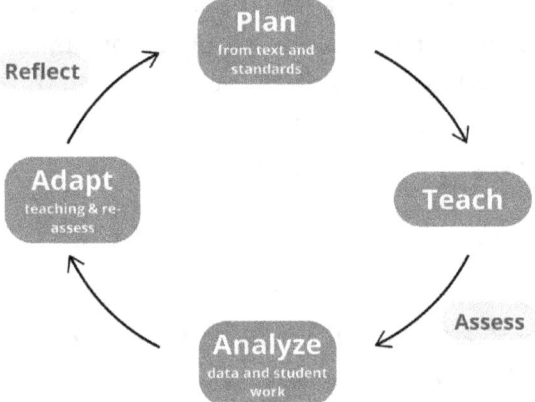

This is a place where Tisha continues to see district leaders miss the mark with their expectations of teachers' lesson plans. There are several lesson plan models that *do* include feedback and reflection as a concrete step for students, but as early as this year (2024) Tisha has reviewed required district lesson plan documents that include *teacher only* feedback or completely skip this step altogether. Additionally, Tisha continues to see news articles with titles like "America's Students Are Falling Behind." We acknowledge there are multiple reasons for students falling behind, including stressful home lives, fewer educational resources available, and lower academic achievement (Abrams, 2024). We also cannot expect students' environments outside of brick-and-mortar classrooms to drastically change and not have a deep impact on what is happening *inside* the classroom. Including student feedback gives teachers an opportunity to see below the surface of a student's performance and creates a safe space for dialogue so students may share more of why they are struggling to complete a checkpoint or piece of content for their portfolio.

This step is crucial and might be the intervention that a student needs to feel more academically confident and successful. Feedback molds future leaders who can sit with their learning experiences and adapt *with* the teacher to meet the end goal. In the learning cycle, feedback is the only way to truly complete the cycle as it prompts authentic self-reflection which is the catalyst for academic and personal growth. In Chapter 8, we will deep dive into the importance of reflection and feedback.

LEARNING PORTFOLIO IDEAS TO EXPLORE

1. Define a purpose: Consider the target audience; confirm application

2. Set a project timeline: Determine checkpoint dates and actionable tasks

3. Curate learning standards: Consider supplemental standards, principles, and types of learning

4. Adapt grading: Review district grading policy, create learning guide or rubric

5. Consider content: Recommend work samples to include, multimedia assets, organization of content

6. Introduce design: Discuss design elements, personal branding

7. Promote feedback: Encourage multiple types, including student-teacher, peer-to-peer, student-parent, student-community

Building on Skills, Not Banning Them

Digital learning portfolios just might be the most underestimated instructional strategy of all time. Remember, digital spaces are curating our content minute-by-minute whether it is posted professionally or personally, and the same is true for students' content (posts, images, and videos). In 2018, The American Academy of Child and Adolescent Psychiatry found that 90% of students between the ages of 13 and 17 have social media, and on average teens spend almost nine hours online each day (American Academy of Child & Adolescent Psychology, 2018). Students consume and create content and are learning the power of sharing information with or without us.

If students already understand the concept of curation, why are we educators not taking the time to cultivate this existing skill (even if in its early stages) and show them how to curate digital information and work samples in a way that will empower and challenge all stakeholders to leverage technology for good? Taking the technology away, "banning" it or blaming it for *all* the issues in schools and with students is a scapegoat tactic used over and over. The *real* solution is finding ways for students to learn how to balance technology skills and use them so integration of responsible digital behaviors into adulthood is less painful for everyone.

Digital learning portfolios deliver a high return on investment when well-planned and intentionally implemented in a classroom or school and transform in tandem with the student's growth. As a bonus, digital learning portfolios naturally incorporate lifelong digital citizenship skills into every facet and step of creation. With advancements in emerging technologies, portfolios will continue to transform into innovative curations showcasing skills and talents far beyond what a typical classroom might be able to, and if students are not prepared, we have no one to blame but ourselves.

**tinyurl.com/
TodaysLearners**

Scan the QR code to access resources associated with this chapter.

Completing the Learning Cycle:
Feedback and Reflection

Standards and Principles Addressed

The content of this chapter aligns with the following standards, indicators, and principles:

ISTE Student Standards

Empowered Learner (1.1.a)

Knowledge Constructor (1.3.a, 1.3.b, 1.3.c, 1.3.d)

Creative Communicator (1.6.a, 1.6.c)

Global Collaborator (1.7.a, 1.7.b, 1.7.c)

ISTE Educator Standards

Leader (2.2.b)

Citizen (2.3.a)

Collaborator (2.4.d)

Designer (2.5.a, 2.5.b)

Facilitator (2.6.a, 2.6.c, 2.6.d)

Analyst (2.7.a, 2.7.b, 2.7.c)

Transformational Learning Principles

Nurture: Connect Learning to Learner, Ensure Equity

Guide: Evaluate Reflection

Empower: Ignite Agency

Reflecting on Feedback

In the current educational environment, feedback is typically short and unspecific: A, B, C, D, F; approaches, meets, exceeds; superior, superior with distinction, excellent, needs attention; or pass, fail. Each level has its own descriptive meaning, but as discussed in Chapter 6, this method of feedback is not specific, personal, or authentic. It is understandable that this type of feedback allows for faster turnaround when reviewing students' assignments and exams when the pressures of covering vast amounts of content and managing the classroom often leave little to no extra time. The pressures to meet learning standards quickly lead to lack of reflection time for both students and teachers, so it is often that students have difficulty identifying points where they need to do more learning or further exploration. This results in essential growth opportunities being missed and an incomplete learning cycle for students (Figure 7.3).

When feedback and reflection processes are conducted efficiently and effectively, students gain clear and actionable insight to guide their learning process. Teachers are not merely instructors but also coaches and mentors, constantly and consistently shaping the student's learning journey. Like a coach, teachers guide students along a path, giving them the information needed to support content learning with practical actions, and revealing the next steps toward feedback and reflection. Teacher feedback, peer feedback, and student reflection are tools that can sharpen and extend learning and progress. However, when this step is overlooked whether due to time constraints or thinking this point in the process is a luxury, a teacher's role can become more managerial, focused solely on sharing information, giving exams, and expecting quick results. By embracing more of a mentoring or coaching approach to content and learning, teachers become true leaders. They create an environment for students to see mistakes as chances to grow, to give patience to themselves and others and to see learning as a process instead of a destination—qualities that will serve students in the future. This one change can create a powerful ripple effect where students, nurtured by leaders, become leaders themselves passing on the value, skill, and love of the learning to others.

For example, Rick's greatest points of growth as a learner occurred when he experienced every step of the entire learning cycle. If feedback was never given, he often failed to reflect and then confused a lack of knowledge with something he did (and would continue to do) wrong. The result was a continuous repeated cycle of mistakes and average work. Without feedback, Rick had no opportunity to reflect or adjust an approach to a problem. When this happens repeatedly to students, it can create feelings of despair and hopelessness.

Managerial mindsets do not focus on feedback or reflection; instead the focus is on task completion and final performance without diving any deeper than the big picture. This cripples growth and makes it impossible to identify strengths and areas for improvement. For many years, Rick truly believed he was not intelligent or clever, not just because of his experience in school with dyslexia but also due to the lack of specific and authentic feedback he unknowingly craved. This caused a shift in his self-worth and became part of the reason he blamed his dyslexia for mistakes or missed opportunities. There were even specific moments when he told himself, "I cannot read a book perfectly and cannot write anything without being criticized, so there is absolutely no way I will ever write a book or anything significant that would help other people."

It was not until he began to surround himself with people who offered constructive feedback and gently encouraged self-reflection that he began to realize his true potential. With their guidance, he began to identify his unique skills and abilities, like communicating and relating to neurodivergent thinkers or recognizing pain points in business or design that others may not see from their vantage point. Tisha recognized something in him that many others had overlooked, likely *because* she is an educator. She provided feedback and support to help Rick recognize the value and skills he brings to problem-solving and innovative thinking that many others do not. Today, as you read these words, you are witnessing something firsthand that Rick once thought was impossible: He wrote a book.

In Chapter 2, "Every Learner Is a Leader," we shared how we are *all* learners; therefore, we are *all* leaders. Setting an example of what a leader is encourages students to believe in their own abilities so that they become empowered to be leaders themselves. This chapter will explore and provide practical ways to fit feedback and reflection strategies into everyday routines, thereby supporting students to consistently develop, grow, and strengthen habits so feedback and reflection become second nature to them. Taking this approach also empowers you as you enrich students' ability to foster a personalized growth mindset and reach their fullest potential.

Understanding Reflection and Feedback

Feedback and reflection are two pivotal components in the learning cycle and can be found overlapping in students' future careers, as well as within problem-solving approaches like design thinking (Chapter 5). Ensuring that feedback and reflection are built into lesson plans and projects significantly enhances learning and teaching outcomes and reveals to even struggling students they have the potential to learn and improve. In education, feedback "helps learners maximize their potential at different stages of training, raise their awareness of strengths and areas for improvement, and identify actions to be taken to improve performance" (Leung et al., 2022). The definition of reflection according to one source is an "instrument by which experiences are translated into dynamic knowledge" (Korthagen, 2001) and per another "a meaning-making process that moves a learner from one experience into the next with a deeper understanding of its relationships with and connections to other experiences and ideas" (University of Connecticut, n.d.).

Within this book, we will define *feedback* as specific, constructive information, advice, or insight, targeted to a teacher or student's learning needs, their performance, improvements, and how to apply the learning. *Reflection* we define as the process by a teacher or student to think deeply about their experiences, actions, and learning by analyzing their work, behaviors, and performance to indicate challenges, areas of success, and where to improve. When used in tandem, feedback and reflection are intertwined processes that drive growth, accountability, and deeper learning. Effective feedback should be specific, timely, and actionable, helping bridge the gap between where students currently are with their performance and their desired target. When feedback is combined with reflection, students and teachers have a chance to take a step back and evaluate the effectiveness of lessons, activities, or actions, internalizing what they learned and adjusting their approach accordingly, resulting in more confident understanding and long-term retention of information.

Feedback and reflection are not easy, and most adults and leaders struggle with this process because it creates vulnerability and the possibility of conflict or discourse. Receiving or giving feedback is one of the hardest aspects of leadership, as it requires us to lead ourselves by taking on the idea that just because we may be experts does not mean we are finished learning. Feedback from students, peers, and parents can offer valuable insight and allow for continuous refinement of pedagogy and instruction. When teachers and students are encouraged to engage in this process, the educational environment becomes an infinite loop of learning, development, and adaptation, building lifelong learners—even beyond graduation.

Student Viewpoints

The impact of feedback and reflection cannot be overstated. If you want to create a truly student-centered learning environment, it would be irresponsible not to include student voices in their own learning cycle. Leaders uplift those around them, and giving students a platform to share their voices is one of the most important ways to model good leadership. Allowing students to share their perspectives on how feedback is communicated creates a culture of ownership and accountability and amplifies their voices. Additionally, it gives you valuable insight into how students perceive feedback, while helping students feel more engaged and empowered. As a result, they become autonomous in self-reflection.

However, feedback must be implemented thoughtfully. As you learned in Chapter 6, missing opportunities to provide timely and specific feedback can be detrimental to a student's growth. We asked Douglas Palmer, Avery Davenport, and other students: "How do you feel when someone gives you feedback on your work/performance?"

> [Feedback] is usually helpful if it is constructive. I do not do well with criticism without purpose or anything negative.
> **—DOUGLAS**

For many, receiving feedback, whether constructive or not, can feel like a personal attack, as we often associate feedback with faults in ourselves rather than opportunities for growth. However, you can transform how you receive and respond to feedback by implementing the Four Agreements (Ruiz, 1997):

- Be impeccable with your word by focusing on the truth within the feedback rather than reacting defensively or internalizing negativity.

- Don't take anything personally; understand that feedback often reflects the other person's perspective or goals, not a judgment of your worth.

- Don't make assumptions about the intention behind the feedback. Instead, seek clarification to ensure you fully understand the message.

- Always do your best by viewing feedback as a tool to refine your efforts and improve, regardless of how it's delivered.

When approached with this mindset, feedback becomes less about fault-finding and more about fostering personal and professional growth.

> [Feedback] is helpful. It used to be very uncomfortable because I took it personally. Knowing better now, I take feedback factually and without emotion. The goal of constructive feedback is never to harm. It is important that we learn how to give feedback that is helpful, not hurtful. **—AVERY**

If feedback is not delivered with care, it can lead to discouragement rather than improvement, mean-spiritedness rather than empathy. This is especially true in educational environments where students are still developing their sense of self and learning to differentiate constructive criticism from other forms of personal disapproval. The results of our informal poll reinforced this message. Overall, students felt that receiving feedback was an experience that they had not had enough of, and they did not feel confident with it initially.

On the other side of the feedback equation, many people hesitate to give feedback because of their uncertainty of how the recipient might react. Don't let uncertainty deter you; simply start small and keep your comments constructive. When Tisha began implementing feedback and reflection with sophomores, juniors, and seniors, she started with simple peer-to-peer comments delivered via the school's learning management system. Immediately, she realized that students were very new to this process, especially students who were used to getting very high grades or remarks from teachers and parents. In the beginning, there were actual tears shed during the process of student-student feedback and reflection. It dawned on Tisha that many high-performing students rarely heard criticisms because they were able to meet the academic expectations of stakeholders easily; meanwhile, low-performing students seemed thrown off by any form of praise for their work, indicating they often were criticized without guidance for improvement.

> [Feedback is] specifically [difficult] when it is negative. It is uncomfortable and scary because the reaction you're going to get is unknown. **—AVERY**

The potential for feedback to be misinterpreted can make the process uncomfortable for both parties.

> If you were to give someone feedback, you wouldn't really know how to tell them without hurting their feelings or making it sound like they didn't do good enough.
> **—DOUGLAS**

To alleviate this uncertainty, it is crucial to approach feedback with empathy, clarity, and an understanding of the individual student's needs. In addition, you must model this so other students can see it in action.

Personalization with feedback is key, and teachers, knowing their students best, can coach others to learn different ways of delivering feedback so the message is received instead of rejected. Each student processes information differently, and each has a unique personality; therefore, feedback that resonates with one student may not have the same impact on another. By empowering students to express their preferred methods of receiving feedback (through written notes, verbal conversations, and structured reflection sessions), you can provide the practice students need to refine this skill into adulthood.

Strategies for Feedback Implementation

Implementing feedback correctly is important because individuals process information in different ways due to diverse learning needs. Some learners may require visuals like diagrams or written comments, whereas others require verbal or hands-on explanations. Providing feedback in ways that meet learners where they are ensures the feedback is not only received but also fully understood and internalized. If feedback is not communicated well, it might lead to confusion, frustration, or demotivation, hindering personal growth and development.

In classrooms, personalized student feedback *can* be a time-consuming process and understandably skipped or even ignored by many. We want to offer implementation strategies that include teacher-student feedback *and* peer-to-peer feedback. This approach takes the feedback and reflection process and puts part of the responsibility onto the learners, helping them to learn how to *provide* good feedback to others for improvement and how to *receive* constructive feedback to improve themselves. For effective teacher-student feedback, try these techniques:

▶▶▶ **Multiple format delivery:** Being flexible with communication to and from students increases the likelihood that the information will be understood and absorbed. Many teachers use learning management systems, secure teacher-student chat capabilities via school email, or approved digital tools to give quick, measurable feedback on projects, writing, or practice exams. Providing feedback in various ways, like written notes, face-to-face conversations, or with the use of digital tools like video or audio recordings, ensures the feedback is accessible and caters to diverse learning styles (Ryan et al., 2019).

▶ *ISTE Student Standards: Creative Communicator 1.6.a; Global Collaborator 1.7.a, 1.7.b. ISTE Educator Standards: Leader 2.2.a; Citizen 2.3.a; Collaborator 2.4.d; Designer 2.5.a; Facilitator 2.6.a; Analyst 2.7.c*

▶ *TLPs: Nurture: Connect Learning to the Leaner, Ensure Equity; Guide: Elevate Reflection, Empower Ignite Agency*

▶ *AIM Framework: Academic Excellence, Interpersonal Skills, Mastery of Self*

▶▶▶ **Two Stars and a Wish:** We all have tendencies to focus on negative feedback and ignore positive comments, often taking the negative feedback with us long after that single moment of communication. The Two Stars and a Wish technique provides a quick, balanced approach by offering two positive comments (the stars) and one suggestion for improvement (a wish). This method is a good way to begin introducing the art of feedback and reflection to students who may never have experienced this in their learning journey. Focusing mostly on the good while giving guidance on one point of improvement creates a positive experience for young learners. By focusing more attention on the good and avoiding being only critical of a student's work, you can create a positive feedback loop that nurtures students' confidence and fosters a desire to continuously improve (Dyer, 2012).

▶ *ISTE Educator Standards: Citizen 2.3.a; Designer 2.5.a; Analyst 2.7.a*

▶ *TLPs: Nurture: Connect Learning to the Learner, Ensure Equity; Guide: Elevate Reflection*

▶ *AIM Framework: Academic Excellence, Interpersonal Skills, Mastery of Self*

▶▶▶ **Regular check-ins:** To create a consistent dialogue between teacher and student, regular check-ins are vital, promoting continuous growth and development and limiting deviation. Many teachers use formative assessment techniques (Chapter 6) to regularly check in with students or even simple techniques, such as students sharing where they are each day on a sticky note. These approaches create a sense of trust between student and teacher that is required before any true reflection and feedback can take place. Instead of giving feedback only at the end of an assignment or after a summative exam, use regular check-ins to offer a continuous conversation where you and your students can ask questions, seek clarification, and adjust their strategies or support in real time. Implementing a scheduled routine where feedback sessions can take place, such as 1:1 student-led conferences, as frequently as you like, helps to strengthen a culture of open communication and keeps students on track and accountable for their personal goals (Marvin, 2024).

▷ *ISTE Educator Standards: Collaborator 2.4.d; Designer 2.5.a; Analyst 2.7.a*

▷ *TLPs: Nurture: Connect Learning to the Leaner; Guide: Elevate Reflection*

▷ *AIM Framework: Interpersonal Skills*

▶▶▶ **Collaborative Sessions:** Transform feedback into an interactive discussion, rather than a one-way information transaction with collaborative feedback sessions whether face-to-face or using digital tools like interactive whiteboards or collaborative documents. Engage with your students by discussing overall projects or daily assignments before you offer feedback. Gaining a clear understanding of a student's intentions, confusion, or thought processes will help you provide tailored and relevant feedback for that student. This approach supports team building among students and creates opportunities for students to help and lead each other. Collaborative feedback empowers students to voice their opinions, ask questions, and take a more active role and responsibility in their learning (Marvin, 2024).

▷ *ISTE Student Standards: Creative Communicator 1.6.a; Global Collaborator 1.7.a, 1.7.b, 1.7.c. ISTE Educator Standards: Designer 2.5.a, 2.5.b; Facilitator 2.6.a; Analyst 2.7.a*

▷ *TLPs: Nurture: Connect Learning to the Learner; Guide: Elevate Reflection*

▷ *AIM Framework: Academic Excellence, Interpersonal Skills*

▶▶▶ **Student self-assessment:** Before students submit work or receive feedback, encourage them to assess their own work first to foster a sense of ownership and responsibility in the learning process. Self-assessment allows each student to critically evaluate their performance and reflect on their strengths and weaknesses. Introducing this to students early on will set them up to expect this as a required part of learning. There are multiple ways to teach students how to do this: brief video reflections, voice notes, or a daily learning journal. It does not need to be lengthy or cumbersome to set up; that would defeat the purpose, causing students to think self-assessment is overly complicated. When students engage in self-assessment, they develop a deeper understanding of the criteria for success. By introducing the student's own perspective, exchange of feedback can be more meaningful and constructive (Yan & Carless, 2021).

▷ *ISTE Student Standards: Empowered Learner 1.1.a. ISTE Educator Standards: Designer 2.5.a; Facilitator 2.6.a*

- *TLPs: Nurture: Connect Learning to the Leaner; Guide: Elevate Reflection; Empower: Ignite Agency*
- *AIM Framework: Academic Excellence, Master of Self*

To nurture effective peer-to-peer feedback, try these techniques:

▶▶▶ **Praise-Question-Suggest:** This technique provides a three-step process to help students learn how to provide feedback to their peers. Students begin with offering positive feedback (praise), then asking a question for clarity or curiosity (question), and finally, offering a potential way to improve (suggest). Teaching students *how* to praise ("Your design on this graphic is very eye-catching."), question ("I'm curious why you chose these colors. Can you tell me more?"), and suggest ("What if you moved this text over a bit and increased the font size for the heading to bring more attention to the message?") provides a model for students to give well-rounded responses and also helps them feel comfortable providing constructive feedback on their peers' work (Grisolía & Serra, 2020).

- *ISTE Student Standard: Global Collaborator 1.7.b. ISTE Educator Standards: Designer 2.5.a, 2.5.b; Facilitator 2.6.d; Analyst 2.7.a*
- *TLPs: Guide: Elevate Reflection; Empower: Ignite Agency*
- *AIM Framework: Interpersonal Skills, Mastery of Self*

▶▶▶ **3 Before Me:** Before submitting any work or approaching the teacher for additional input, have students first seek feedback from three of their peers. This technique promotes collaboration, independence, and critical thinking, as students learn to approach and rely on their peers for trustful and beneficial guidance before turning a project or assignment in to the teacher. Tisha implemented this approach with her students to develop a classroom culture where everyone was a learner *and* a leader. Additionally, it helped reduce Tisha's grading workload because students were able to refine their work and catch smaller mistakes before final submission. This method teaches students through multiple perspectives before requesting further clarification from the teacher (Nollmeyer et al., 2018).

- *ISTE Student Standards: Creative Communicator 1.6.d; Global Collaborator 1.7.b. ISTE Educator Standards: Designer 2.5.a; Facilitator 2.6.d; Analyst 2.7.a*
- *TLPs: Guide: Elevate Reflection; Empower: Ignite Agency*
- *AIM Framework: Interpersonal Skills, Mastery of Self*

▶▶▶ **Peer feedback conferences:** Conferences do not have to be all-encompassing events for students to benefit. Peer feedback conference time is a dynamic and interactive way for students to engage in conversational feedback by discussing their work face-to-face with their peers. Students can ask questions, clarify misunderstandings, and begin deeper dialogue with each other about content, assignments, and learning. This conference-style approach strengthens collaboration and allows for the exchange of ideas and understanding more thoroughly than through written comments (Cronin, 2016).

▶ *ISTE Student Standards: Creative Communicator 1.6.a, 1.6.d; Global Collaborator 1.7.b. ISTE Educator Standards: Citizen 2.3.a; Designer 2.5.a; Facilitator 2.6.d*

▶ *TLPs: Nurture Connect Learning to the Learner; Guide: Elevate Reflection; Empower: Ignite Agency*

▶ *AIM Framework: Academic Excellence, Interpersonal Skills, Mastery of Self*

▶▶▶ **Review rotations:** Receiving feedback from a variety of peers by rotating feedback partners or groups offers a diverse range of perspectives. This may be seen as a more traditional method where students pass their papers to the right or the left for grading, but teachers can improve this process by giving students guidance on what they are looking for, increase the number of reviewers, and supply a guide with wording and ideas previously discussed as a whole group. By introducing a structured peer review rotation, students receive input from multiple sources, helping students see their work from different angles (Sanako Blog, 2024).

▶ *ISTE Student Standards: Creative Communicator 1.6.a, 1,6.d; Global Collaborator 1.7.b. ISTE Educator Standards: Collaborator 2.4.d; Designer 2.5.a, 2.5.b; Facilitator 2.6.d; Analyst 2.7.a*

▶ *TLPs: Guide: Elevate Reflection; Empower: Ignite Agency*

▶ *AIM Framework: Interpersonal Skills, Mastery of Self*

▶▶▶ **Gallery walks:** Turn your classroom into an interactive display by showcasing students' work on the walls. Then have peers stationed around the room, leaving constructive feedback on sticky notes. This visual activity gives students the opportunity to engage in a variety of work, offering concise and targeted feedback. Turn this into a digital gallery walk by using QR codes that take students to curated groups of information, graphic designs, student videos, audio summaries, or digital slide decks. Learning walks promote an open and collaborative environment where students benefit from multiple perspectives and learn how to demonstrate individual skills and talents (Allen & Larmer, 2013).

- *ISTE Student Standards: Creative Communicator 1.6.d; Global Collaborator 1.7.a, 1.7.b. ISTE Educator Standards: Citizen 2.3.a; Collaborator 2.4.d; Designer 2.5.a; Facilitator 2.6.a, 2.6.d; Analyst 2.7.a, 2.7.b*

- *TLPs: Nurture: Connect Learning to the Learner, Ensure Equity; Guide: Elevate Reflection, Empower Ignite Agency*

- *AIM Framework: Academic Excellence, Interpersonal Skills, Mastery of Self*

Strategies for Reflection Implementation

Reflection goes beyond task completion; it invites students to analyze their ideas, think about problem-solving strategies, and review their work in a way that is different from just receiving a letter or number grade. Student reflection requires learners to flex their critical thinking muscles and gives them time to think deeply about their experiences, identifying what has been learned, what needs more attention, and where to apply. By recognizing connections between their reflective insights and their broader learning goals, students can strategically incorporate what they have learned into future tasks, projects, and challenges. For instance, they could apply a newly discovered study technique to a different subject or adapt a successful collaborative approach to another group setting. When reflection is immersed into classrooms, learners come to realize their strengths, as well as areas to improve, and are better able to meet their own goals.

It is important to implement reflection effectively and efficiently for all learners. Done correctly, reflection has the potential to enhance the transfer of knowledge and skills across different contexts. Through reflection, every experience can transform into a valuable learning experience that shapes future learning and decision-making and is crucial for long-term success.

Remember, however, that any time students are involved, one size does *not* work for all. Be mindful of unique situations that may need some adjustments and be open to awareness of any strategies that might disrupt the development of this skill. Our words hold more power than we even know and something shared may not initially feel impactful to a teacher or peer might hold a lot of weight for a particular student.

Following are five ideas to help students learn and improve reflection skills no matter their learning preferences:

▶▶▶ **Learning journals:** Tracking feedback given or received over time helps students reflect on their growth and development. By maintaining a journal, students document how the feedback they received influenced their work habits, changes with work samples, and how the feedback helped to develop critical thinking skills. This approach continuously encourages ongoing reflection of the feedback process as an integral part of learning (Rogers, 2023).

▸ *ISTE Student Standards: Empowered Learner 1.1.a; Creative Communicator 1.6.a. ISTE Educator Standards: Designer 2.5.a; Facilitator 2.6.a, 2.6.d*

▸ *TLPs: Nurture: Connect Learning to the Learner; Guide: Elevate Reflection, Empower Ignite Agency*

▸ *AIM Framework: Academic Excellence, Mastery of Self*

▶▶▶ **Reflective dialogue with the teacher:** A follow-up conversation with their teacher provides students with an opportunity to clarify any misunderstandings they may have and to discuss how to implement any suggestions given. Conversations between teacher and student create a supportive environment to encourage question asking, feedback exploration, and time to clarify expectations or misunderstandings. Additionally, dialogue prepares students for self-advocacy in the present and future. This strategy helps students to feel heard and be truly seen, as well as reinforces the value of reflection (Hattie & Timperley, 2007).

▸ *ISTE Student Standards: Empowered Learner 1.1.a. ISTE Educator Standards: Facilitator 2.6.d; Analyst 2.7.a*

▸ *TLPs: Nurture: Connect Learning to the Learner; Guide: Elevate Reflection; Empower: Ignite Agency*

▸ *AIM Framework: Academic Excellence, Interpersonal Skills, Mastery of Self*

▶▶▶ **Reflective questioning:** Leading students with reflective questions is a powerful way to support them in learning how to effectively and efficiently reflect on feedback. Questions like "What did I do well?" "Where could I improve?" and "How can I apply this feedback moving forward?" teach students to critically analyze feedback rather than passively receive it. Introducing reflective questions helps students understand how to reflect and creates an active and deeper learning experience (Brookfield, 2017).

▸ *ISTE Student Standard: Empowered Learner 1.1.a. ISTE Educator Standards: Designer 2.5.a; Facilitator 2.6.a; Analyst 2.7.a*

▸ *TLPs: Nurture: Connect Learning to the Learner; Guide: Elevate Reflection*

▸ *AIM Framework: Master of Self*

▶▶▶ **Reflection template:** Help students structure their thinking when reflecting on feedback. Using school-approved devices and digital tools, introduce a reflection template (FIGURE 8.1) to assist students through a systematic approach. This template should offer prompts for identifying strengths, areas for improvement, and action steps. Space for an emotional check-in will help all parties identify trends and request additional support for the student. When students feel overwhelmed by feedback, providing a template gives them a clear overall picture and helps them curate their experiences and growth over time (Gibbs, 1988).

▸ *ISTE Student Standard: Empowered Learner 1.1.a. ISTE Educator Standards: Designer 2.5.a, 2.5.b; Facilitator 2.6.a; Analyst 2.7.a*

▸ *TLPs: Nurture: Connect Learning to the Learner; Guide: Elevate Reflection*

▸ *AIM Framework: Mastery of Self*

▶▶▶ **Reflection prompts:** Enabling a growth mindset in students is one of the most powerful results of feedback and is achieved by adjusting the idea of feedback from criticism to opportunity. Implementing reflection prompts like "What new skills can I develop from this feedback?" or "How can I address the challenges highlighted in this feedback?" direct students to look at feedback with a positive and forward-thinking attitude. This strategy shifts the focus from mistakes to actions for growth, thereby supporting resilience and motivation to improve (Dweck, 2006).

▸ *ISTE Student Standard: Empowered Learner 1.1.a. ISTE Educator Standards: Designer 2.5.a; Facilitator 2.6.a; Analyst 2.7.a*

▸ *TLPs: Nurture: Connect Learning to the Learner; Guide: Elevate Reflection*

▸ *AIM Framework: Interpersonal Skills, Mastery of Self*

You can access templates for learning journals and the reflection template by scanning the QR code at the end of the chapter.

Teacher-Student dialogue	Student self-reflection	Confidence building prompts
"Tell me something you're proud of about this project/lesson" "What part of your work do you feel best represents your skills or growth?" "If you could give advice to someone just starting this project/lesson, what would it be?" "How do you believe this project/lesson connects to your bigger goals?" "What range of emotions did you experience during the learning and how did you manage them?"	What did I learn during this lesson/project that was surprising to me? Which parts were the most challenging? How did I overcome any difficulty? How could I improve my process next time? How do I feel about the effort I put into this work? What feedback did I receive and how did I use it to make my project/lesson better?	I am proud of myself because_____. One strength I used during this lesson/project was _____. One way I will apply what I've learned is _____. One challenge I faced was _____ and I overcame it by _____. This says _____ about my ability to handle difficult situations. The part of the project/lesson that makes me feel the most confident is _____ because _____ _____

FIGURE 8.1
A reflection template

Infinite Feedback, Transformative Growth

Teachers play a crucial leadership role in the learning cycle by modeling the importance of feedback and reflection. They demonstrate that learning is an ongoing journey where mistakes are not failures but opportunities for growth. As we've discussed, feedback and reflection are essential for completing the learning cycle and fostering continuous growth, resilience, and deeper understanding. When students witness their teachers seeking feedback and reflecting on their own practices, students are more likely to adopt these habits themselves. This leadership cultivates a classroom culture that values continuous improvement, empowering students to take risks, reflect on their progress, and engage actively in their learning.

Teaching students how to give and receive feedback in a specific, constructive, and timely manner helps them approach feedback with an open mindset. This prevents them from viewing feedback as criticism and instead encourages self-improvement without becoming overly self-critical or discouraged.

The impact of mastering feedback and reflection extends well beyond the classroom. Students who develop these skills carry them into higher education and their careers, where they are better equipped to navigate challenges, adapt to change, and continuously grow. As future leaders, they will pass on these practices, fostering both personal and professional development, and embracing a lifelong journey of learning.

Scan the QR code to access resources associated with this chapter.

**tinyurl.com/
TodaysLearners**

CHAPTER 9

Teaching Beyond Tradition

Standards and Principles Addressed

The content of this chapter aligns with the following standards, indicators, and principles:

ISTE Student Standards

Empowered Learner (1.1.a, 1.1.b, 1.1.c, 1.1.d)

Digital Citizen (1.2.a, 1.2.b, 1.2.c, 1.2.d)

Knowledge Constructor (1.3.a, 1.3.b, 1.3.c, 1.3.d)

Innovative Designer (1.4.a, 1.4.b, 1.4.c, 1.4.d)

Computational Thinker (1.5.a, 1.5.b, 1.5.c, 1.5.b)

Creative Communicator (1.6.a, 1.6.b, 1.6.c, 1.6.d)

Global Collaborator (1.7.a, 1.7.b, 1.7.c, 1.7.d)

ISTE Educator Standards

Learner (2.1.a, 2.1.b, 2.1.c)

Leader (2.2.a, 2.2.b, 2.2.c)

Citizen (2.3.a, 2.3.b, 2.3.c, 2.3.d)

Collaborator (2.4.a, 2.4.b, 2.4.c, 2.4.d)

Designer (2.5.a, 2.5.b, 2.5.c)

Facilitator (2.6.a, 2.6.b, 2.6.c, 2.6.d)

Analyst (2.7.a, 2.7.b, 2.7.c)

Transformational Learning Principles

Nurture: Cultivate Belongining, Connect Learning to Learner, Ensure Equity

Guide: Spark Curiosity, Develop Expertise, Elevate Reflection

Empower: Prioritize Authentic Experiences, Ignite Agency

The Evolving Landscape of Teaching

Like technology, teaching continues to change and transform. Many middle school and high school veteran teachers can recall a time when work hours were seven hours; the workload included five classes with two to three preps and at least one planning period, no standardized tests, no extra duties before or after school, and only one staff or department meeting per month. Teachers work eight hours or *more* today, not including the time they put in after students go home or the work that follows them home. They have six to seven classes with four to five preps and one planning period *or less*; three or more standardized practice tests per year; the management of students' Individualized Education Plans (IEPs), accommodations, and support meetings; and morning, lunch, or afternoon duty, which can take an additional hour from their day. Staff meetings, department meetings, and leadership meetings now occur as often as once a week, which must be before or after school or during the one planning period teachers have without students present. Teachers have been trying to explain the increased demand to parents and community members for years because, in addition, teachers are required to train for active shooter drills, social-emotional learning, first aid, and cardiopulmonary resuscitation (CPR); to design curriculum maps; to create and manage online classrooms and grade books; and ensure parent meetings and communications are consistent.

On top of *that*, many schools and districts have local requirements, such as technology integration, club or class sponsorship, and coaching duties, and every teacher we have spoken with has acknowledged that student behavior is one of the most challenging aspects of teaching today.

If you are reading this, you are aware of the nationwide challenges to keep teachers in teaching positions due to low compensation, unrealistic expectations, nonexistent work-life balance, complex leadership, and lack of workplace flexibility (Betkowski, 2024). Currently, it seems that every news source reports only the negative aspects of education, and there is an overlying consensus that teacher recruitment can take districts and schools only so far. The real challenge is *retaining* teachers, and the best way to do that is to address the challenges listed above and maybe share them more often with those who have not been paying attention.

While we *completely agree* that the education system and its support for teachers and students is lacking, there is a sliver of hope in the research and educators we have found. There *are* fully dedicated teachers who are *all in* and more passionate than ever about teaching and learning. Teachers *are* seeking support and knowledge to streamline their workload and have surrounded themselves with other innovative educators to learn future skills necessary for themselves and their students. Teachers are persevering despite the obstacles they face each day. They are showing up for their students, their teams, and themselves.

This chapter recognizes that teaching is not an easy profession, and some of the calls to action we have shared in previous chapters may not work for every classroom or environment. However, we are asking you to consider that the change must start with each of us in the small, quiet moments as we prepare our classrooms before the first bell, as we greet each student when they file in from the previous class period, and when a challenging change is enforced and implemented by someone who is not or has never been a teacher.

The transformation in teaching begins with the transformation within each of *us*. Our students become our mirrors reflecting our behaviors, and we should remind ourselves that even if they seem not to be paying attention or acting as if they do not care, they are still silently absorbing the energy and attitudes we bring to them each day. If *we* believe in their ability to be learners and leaders, they, too, will believe this to be true.

Characteristics of Transformational Teaching

If you have read this far, you are already on your way to transforming your teaching practice and setting your students up for a future of success. Each of the previous chapters was written with the idea that a teacher (or student) could pick up this book, turn to any chapter or page, and begin implementing ideas and strategies to empower learning that transforms leadership. By now, you recognize the importance of understanding how students think and are somewhat familiar with transformative teaching practices. How do you begin transforming your own practice?

Although there are no specific steps to follow, research does confirm particular methods have a greater impact than others and are "student approved." A study in 2013 revealed which transformational teaching practices students see as beneficial to their learning (Agommuoh, & Ifeanacho, 2013):

- peer tutoring
- simulations
- team teaching
- brainstorming
- experiential learning
- cooperative learning
- cognitive apprenticeship
- discovery learning
- inquiry learning
- role play

Many of these strategies should sound familiar from previous chapters. In addition, the same study found that students understand that these transformational teaching practices help equip them with the skills needed to "solve life problems and contribute to the development and growth of society" (Agommuoh & Ifeanacho, 2013).

To transform teaching, educators should aim to transform passive students into engaged learners and leaders. Doing this must include more authentic practices combined with traditional assessments. As you remember from Chapter 6, using only traditional standardized assessments does not entirely reflect a student's ability and creates an environment in which students are taught that learning is solely a way to consume or receive information. By combining traditional assessment data with authentic experiences that include student feedback and reflection (Chapter 8), you will help students recognize that learning is a balance between receiving and contributing.

Meaningful learning experiences, reflective practices that support student reflection (Chapter 8), and student agency and leadership (Chapter 3) are good places to start implementing a transformational practice.

Additionally, as a new teacher, Tisha allowed her students to share their feedback with her during Feedback Focus moments. These moments included time for them to share how they learn best, their philosophies about technology and technology for learning, and questions on what they felt might not be working with classroom procedures or classwork. These moments taught Tisha a lot about how to gracefully receive feedback from students whose words are not always delivered "gently." Begin teaching your students how to communicate constructive feedback and how to receive feedback (Chapter 8) *before* implementing your own Feedback Focus sessions into the classroom culture. Scheduling feedback after a lesson, project, or semester is just as important as the questions you ask students. Remember, what works for one group of kids may not always work for another. Be open and willing to adjust Feedback Focus moments so the intent (student voice) matches the result (improvement with instruction and learning). For some sample Feedback Focus questions, scan the QR code at the end of this chapter.

To help you get started, here are some ideas that have worked for other teachers:

> I weave in student leadership opportunities into my English Language Arts classes. Whether it be speaker/leader roles in table groups or discussion leaders during Socratic seminars. My entire goal is to provide students with scaffolds and support

so they may slowly be removed so students are, in fact, taking ownership of their learning. I move them away from the mindset of "is this for a grade?" which does take more time with some groups, but also is a necessary step for them to become capable learners and continue developing as such. I often discover students have specific skills and over time with encouragement they become the class experts. I like to showcase these students as they teach me something new so I can model continuous learning and curiosity.

—LAURA STEINBRINK, TWENTY-NINE-YEAR VETERAN TEACHER

Because of the nature of our class, we hold a lot of discussions about various topics. Then we complete reflection activities that accompany the discussions which helps kids to analyze their own behaviors, seek reasoning for them, and make changes where necessary. Reflections also encourage students to [learn to] identify problems and find solutions, which helps them to apply the process personally, socially, and within our community. In my experience, kids learn better when they are guided to think and see the purpose for their learning. When they can see the problem and recognize the need for the solution, they are more likely to intrinsically begin building the skills necessary to be a leader and problem solver.

—STACIE WHITE, TWENTY-YEAR VETERAN TEACHER

One of my favorite ways to encourage entrepreneurial skills was to do a classroom economy. Students paid bills, received paychecks, and learned to balance wants and needs. You must create an environment where it is safe to fail. Sometimes that means students have to see you fail and reflect on your past failures, explaining what happened and what could have gone better. Students should not be punished for failure and should learn that it is perfectly okay.

—RACHEL MEDRANO, SEVENTEEN YEARS IN EDUCATION

Sparking Conversation

Sitting with a group of teachers, you will discover quickly that many did not pursue teaching for the money (although they are worthy of millions). They became teachers for a multitude of other reasons: to pay forward what a teacher did for them, to mentor other teachers and students, to teach students how to read or pass an exam, or even to continue a legacy started by a family member years before.

Through the years of teaching and learning, I have fallen in love with helping students become healthy productive adults who will add to our society in a positive manner and be successful in their own way. **—STACIE**

Throughout this book, we have shared how important reflection strategies and their implementation are to the learning process to drive student success. Time for educators to reflect on their instruction is just as important, and it will directly affect the success of their students. As busy educators work from sunup to sundown meeting the expectations set forth upon them, it is easy to lose sight of how to complete the last step of the learning cycle—reflection—for students and for themselves. Instructional strategies that create time and space for students to explore and engage in authentic learning experiences are ever-changing and transforming. What works for one educator and class might not be the best approach for another. What works with one class of students one year might not be the right fit for the next group. The same is true for teachers, especially as they work to balance challenging circumstances (large class sizes, limited time, increased responsibilities) alongside required standards. It is important for all stakeholders, especially school leaders, to recognize these real challenges and understand that not prioritizing time for teachers to converse, brainstorm, reflect, and explore will directly affect students' motivation and success in the classroom. If teachers are running on empty without time for complete, daily conversations with colleagues and experts in their field, it will take a toll.

A teacher's main goal is to impact, inspire, and lead students to do great things, and to do that they must keep themselves inspired and motivated. This can be quite challenging, but one of the best ways to do this is to make time to have conversations with your team, whether in the school hallway or digital spaces. For some, these discussions are coordinated by their school district; during required professional learning community (PLC) meetings, educators gather to improve their teaching practices and create learning environments that improve overall student success (PowerSchool, 2023). These gatherings are scheduled consistently and often built into a school's master schedule to create the time necessary for teachers to sit, uninterrupted, and operate so everyone has a chance to share or ask questions. There may be an agenda, but there is not a set of learning objectives to master as found in professional development workshops or "lunch and learns." While some of the same topics or questions surrounding students' success may come up in a professional development session, the aim of the PLC is to implement agreed upon tasks or action items that move students closer to the end goal.

But what about teachers who have not been given the gift of time for PLC meetings or common planning periods to plan and brainstorm together? Informal conversations might be the only interaction teachers get with each other in their school, but these small encounters can reignite passion, provide purpose, and become the birthplace for new ideas that support teacher and student success. Instructional coaching or technology coaching sessions might be a great place to recapture time for teachers to connect and begin conversations of reflection and innovative ideas, but even having to serve the same hallway duty timeframe might spark a collaboration or project-based learning activity that challenges both the teachers and the students to learn side-by-side.

The PLC Continuous Improvement Cycle (FIGURE 9.1) looks similar to the design thinking model (Chapter 5) and the learning cycle: It guides teachers to apply insights, gather evidence, develop and implement strategies, and analyze what worked and what did not (PowerSchool, 2023). All three models demonstrate the importance of conversation among educators, requiring them to come together and share their qualitative and quantitative data with others, showing evidence, explaining which strategies work and how they might be improved. Additionally, teachers can then take time to implement new strategies and come back together to analyze their experiences. You do not need a special day, time, or room set aside for this process to be successful. These conversations can happen at the copy machine, in the lunchroom, or in a digital space no matter the day or time.

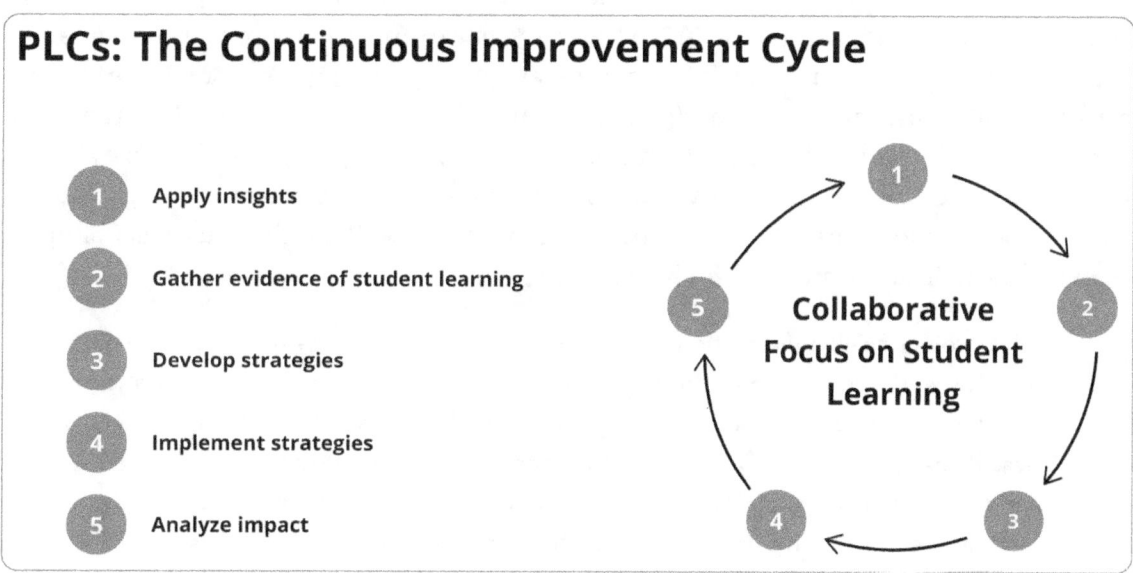

FIGURE 9.1
The PLC Continuous Improvement Cycle

Hearing from Teachers Like You

Take a closer look at the AIM Framework in Chapter 2, this time reviewing each stake-holder's focal points of success. The educator is the only stakeholder aiming for students to achieve *all* the skills and characteristics listed in the framework. Educators know that academic excellence is vital, but they also see how interpersonal skills and self-mastery places each student on a path that leads to continued success past high school graduation. Sometimes it is best to hear from teachers directly to learn *how* they are transforming their teaching, the achievements they see from their students, and how that inspires them. With that in mind, we asked a group of teachers to share some of their best activities and projects that illustrate student leadership, entrepreneurship, critical thinking, and problem solving in action.

Michelle Adkins taught for seventeen years in Kansas before moving to Texas. While not all states or districts allow lesson delivery flexibility, she quickly discovered that she loved integrating learning standards into lessons across the curriculum and meeting students' individual needs in the best way possible. She saw firsthand how this instructional approach increased engagement and impact, helping students retain knowledge more effectively. "This freedom lends itself to [creating] great lessons," she said. One of her favorite lessons was for first grade STEM/STEAM. Students read *My Robot* by Eve Bunting and were learning 3D shapes in math. Michelle and her teaching partner, Staci Hansen, designed a lesson that included the story, math, and science to help students learn about robots. The problem for students was to design a robot using real-world recycled material. They were given a design sheet that included the criteria for their robot and had to use only what was provided by teachers. Once complete, they wrote a story about their robot based on the story by Eve Bunting and the information they learned about what robots can do in the real world. The Robot Project is available for you to use; simply scan the QR code at the end of this chapter.

> This project challenged students with design and perseverance when something did not work the first time. I observed lots of student collaboration, encouragement of each other, and the joy as they discovered their creativity. And their writing was amazing because it was personal to them. I have adapted this for younger students, and it could be used with older students, too. District Media and Technology specialists can help if you adjust this and use a 3D printer. Projects like this push boundaries and become a student favorite.
> **—MICHELLE**

During our conversation, Laura asked us, "Have you heard of reciprocal teaching?" Reciprocal teaching is an instructional procedure designed to teach students cognitive strategies to improve reading comprehension (Rosenshine & Meister, 1994). She then explained how she put the technique to work. (You can find Laura's resources by scanning the QR code at the end of this chapter.)

> Teachers and students take turns leading discussions about a particular text and focusing on four comprehension strategies: predicting, clarifying, questioning, and summarizing. Knowing this strategy, I look for ways to use it with my AP Language and Composition students who grapple with more complex texts and learn to annotate. I have my students do reciprocal annotating using an online curation tool, keeping the design as simple as possible so they will focus on their content instead of the design. Student groups were assigned to independently read a range of text, sharing annotations digitally and discussing why they were important, picking the top three annotations to curate in real time. Groups then designate a leader to speak and validate why their annotations were important and answer student questions over their assigned section."   **—LAURA**

Last, but not least, Stacie White shared one of her main projects: the Employee Choice Award. This project encompasses the majority of the skills listed in the AIM Framework and drives Stacie's passion for helping students become "healthy and productive adults who positively impact society." All of Stacie's resources are available for you via QR code at the end of this chapter.

> Students prepare and plan for [the Employee Choice Award] the entire year. Everything we do is geared toward preparing students for this one competition. To do this, I include a study of the book *7 Habits of Highly Effective Teens*, community service projects, financial planning and budgeting projects, resume building, and intense interview practice. Students compile approximately thirteen documents over the year into a digital portfolio that is then sent out to a panel of community members who judge the student portfolios and logo designs and interview each student. Finalists receive a monetary prize toward items to help them pursue their chosen career. Douglas Palmer won in 2024 and received an exercise bike, a basketball goal, and a basketball that counts the number of shots and dribbles and sends the information to his phone for analysis. This project has been eye-opening as it gives *everyone*—no matter background or ability—an equal opportunity to actively learn skills that are proven to help them succeed.   **—STACIE**

These are only a few examples of teachers transforming teaching and learning with projects that push their students out of their comfort zones to learn entrepreneurial and leadership skills that will carry them into a future of confident problem-solving and innovation. There is no right or wrong place to start teaching beyond tradition. *Right now* is the best time to find the ideas in this book that resonate or inspire you. *Little by little* is the only way to grow instructional practices, and those little steps each day will lead to *incredible changes* in your students, your classrooms, and in you!

Being Curious, Solving Problems, and Loving Learning

Shifting limited beliefs is only possible when we allow ourselves to sit in the discomfort of a new idea or thought. We cannot do this alone, and for many teachers who give every second of their day to their jobs it can feel impossible to find time to connect with other educators. Functioning in isolation or doing the same thing we have always done does not serve our students and will keep *us* in a loop that limits our beliefs and growth—personally, and professionally.

If your end goal is to create evolving learners and leaders, *you* must embody those characteristics, so every interaction allows your students to *see* what being a lifelong learner and leader looks like. Our attitudes and mindsets toward learning, new technologies, and overall educational beliefs directly affect our students. Sitting in the energy of fixed beliefs creates a classroom culture where this is expressed in our words and actions. As a result, we develop students who reflect a fixed mindset back to us. Teacher mindset beliefs predict student achievement and motivation above and beyond any other characteristic (Armstrong, 2019). If you want students who love learning, are eager to solve problems, and show up consistently curious, you must first become what you want to see in them. They are learners on the path to leadership, but so are *you*.

tinyurl.com/ TodaysLearners

Scan the QR code to access resources associated with this chapter.

References

Aarons, G. A. (2006, August 1). Transformational and transactional leadership: Association with attitudes toward evidence-based practice. *Psychiatric Services, 57*(8), 1153–1161. https://doi.org/10.1176/ps.2006.57.8.1162

Abatayo, J. (2014, April 14). *Authentic assessment vs. performance assessment: A tale of two scales* [Transcript, Slides]. Prezi. https://prezi.com/kcmyxssim0dt/authentic-assessment-vs-performance-assessment-a-tale-of-t

Abrams, Z. (2024, April 1) America's students are falling behind. Here's how to reimagine the classroom. *Monitor on Psychology. 55*(3), 54. https://www.apa.org/monitor/2024/04/psychologists-help-transform-school-experience

ADDA Editorial Team. (2023, July 17). *Top 5 potential benefits of ADHD for employees.* Attention Deficit Disorder Association. https://add.org/benefits-of-adhd-employees

Adobe. (2018). *Creative problem-solving in schools: Essential skills today's students need for jobs in tomorrow's age of automation.* Adobe Educate. https://cps.adobeeducate.com/GlobalStudy

Agommuoh, P. C., & Ifeanacho, A. O. (2013). Secondary school students' assessment of innovative teaching strategies in enhancing achievement in physics and mathematics. *IOSR Journal of Research & Method in Education (IOSR-JRME), 3*(5), 6–11.

Alam, M. (2024). *5 essential innovation thinking skills you need to succeed.* IdeaScale. https://ideascale.com/blog/innovation-thinking-skills

Allen, J. L. C., & Larmer, J. (2013, September 9). Using gallery walks for critique & revision in PBL. *PBLWorks, Buck Institute for Education.* https://www.pblworks.org/blog/using-gallery-walks-critique-revision-pbl

American Academy of Child & Adolescent Psychology. (2018, March). *Social media and teens.* https://www.aacap.org/AACAP/Families_and_Youth/Facts_for_Families/FFF-Guide/Social-Media-and-Teens-100.aspx

Armstrong, K. (2019, October 29). Carol Dweck on how growth mindsets can bear fruit in the classroom. *Observer.* https://www.psychologicalscience.org/observer/dweck-growth-mindsets

Atlanta Public Schools. (n.d.). *Profile of a graduate.* https://www.atlantapublicschools.us/Page/70987

Bailey, J. M., & Guskey, T. R. (2001). *Implementing student-led conferences.* Corwin Press.

Banks, J. A. (2015). *Cultural diversity and education: Foundations, curriculum, and teaching.* Routledge.

Bencivenga, A. (2006, April 4). *A shared vision: Reading parents' minds.* Edutopia. https://www.edutopia.org/shared-vision

BerkleyExecEd. (n.d.). *Creating a purpose-driven personal brand.* https://executive.berkeley.edu/thought-leadership/blog/creating-purpose-driven-personal-brand

Betkowski, A. (2024, March 26). Why are teachers quitting?. *Teaching in Purple, Grand Canyon University.* https://www.gcu.edu/blog/teaching-school-administration/why-are-teachers-quitting

Bidwell, A. (2014, February 27). The history of Common Core State Standards. *U.S. News.* https://www.usnews.com/news/special-reports/articles/2014/02/27/the-history-of-common-core-state-standards

Blakemore, E. (2023, October 4). *In early 1800s American classrooms, students governed themselves.* History. https://www.history.com/news/in-early-1800s-american-classrooms-students-governed-themselves

Brookfield, S. D. (2017). *Becoming a critically reflective teacher* (2nd ed.). Jossey-Bass.

Burch, K. (2023, December 11). *10 surprising benefits of having ADHD.* Verywell Health. https://www.verywellhealth.com/benefits-of-adhd-strengths-and-superpowers-5210520

Clarke, A. (Host). (2023, December 4). Revelling in recognition: Why entrepreneurs should celebrate success. *Real World Entrepreneurship* [Audio podcast]. https://realworldentrepreneurship.com/2023/12/04/celebrate-success

Cody, S. (2023, September 15). Council post: How to shift your team's mindset from "yes, but" to "yes, and." *Forbes.* https://www.forbes.com/sites/forbesbusinesscouncil/2023/09/15/how-to-shift-your-teams-mindset-from-yes-but-to-yes-and

Cornell University. (n.d.). *Digital portfolios (digication).* Center for Teaching Innovation. https://teaching.cornell.edu/learning-technologies/collaboration-tools/digital-portfolios-digication

Cornell University. (n.d.). *Sense of belonging.* https://diversity.cornell.edu/belonging/sense-belonging

Costa, A. L., & Kallick, B. (Eds.). (2008). *Learning and leading with habits of mind: 16 essential characteristics for success.* ASCD.

Coursera Staff. (2024, February 26). *What are leadership skills, and why are they important?* Coursera. https://www.coursera.org/articles/leadership-skills

Cronin, A. (2016, July 8). *Student-led conferences: Resources for educators.* Edutopia. https://www.edutopia.org/blog/student-led-conferences-resources-ashley-cronin

Cropley, D. H. (2016). Creativity in engineering. In G. E. Corazza, & S. Agnoli (Eds.), *Multidisciplinary contributions to the science of creative thinking* (pp. 155–173). Springer. https://doi.org/10.1007/978-981-287-618-8_10

Danielson, C. (2007). *Enhancing professional practice: A framework for teaching.* ASCD.

Davis, N. (2009, July 8). The Constructivist Theory – Yeah, so, what's that? The theory explained!. *Nina's Arena-Teaching & Learning in the Australian Primary Classroom.* https://ninadavis.me/2009/07/08/the-constructivist-theory-yeah-so-whats-that-the-theory-explained

de Bono, E. (1999). *Six thinking hats* (revised edition). Back Bay Books.

Driscoll, M. P. (2002). *How people learn (and what technology might have to do with it).* ERIC Clearinghouse on Information and Technology. https://files.eric.ed.gov/fulltext/ED470032.pdf

Dunlea, M. (2019, September 4). *Every student matters: Cultivating belonging in the classroom.* Edutopia. https://www.edutopia.org/article/every-student-matters-cultivating-belonging-classroom

Dunne, K. (n.d.). *SWOT analysis.* MindTools. https://www.mindtools.com/amtbj63/swot-analysis

Dweck, C. S. (2006). *Mindset: The new psychology of success.* Random House.

Dyer, K. (2012, December 10). *27 easy formative assessment strategies for gathering evidence of student learning.* NWEA. https://www.nwea.org/blog/2024/27-easy-formative-assessment-strategies-for-gathering-evidence-of-student-learning

Dyer, K. (2024, May 21). *27 easy formative assessment strategies for gathering evidence of student learning.* NWEA. https://www.nwea.org/blog/2024/27-easy-formative-assessment-strategies-for-gathering-evidence-of-student-learning

Eccles, J. S., Barber, B. L., Stone, M., & Hunt, J. (2003). Extracurricular activities and adolescent development. *Journal of Social Issues, 59*(4), 865–889.

Ertmer, P. A., & Newby, T. J. (1993). Behaviorism, cognitivism, constructivism: Comparing critical features from an instructional design perspective. *Performance Improvement Quarterly, 6*(4), 50–72.

Facing History & Ourselves. (2020, May 12). *Socratic seminar.* https://www.facinghistory.org/resource-library/socratic-seminar

Faisal, S. (2024, September 30). *Framework for problem-solving: 5 best examples for product teams.* https://userpilot.com/blog/problem-solving-framework

Fitzpatrick, D. (2024, June 16). 5 questions for ambitious leaders driving change in education. *Forbes.* https://www.forbes.com/sites/danfitzpatrick/2024/06/16/5-questions-for-ambitious-leaders-driving-change-in-education/

Friend, M., & Cook, L. (1992). *Interactions: Collaboration skills for school professionals.* Longman Publishing Group.

Friesen, S., & Scott, D. (2013, June). Inquiry-based learning: A review of the research literature. Alberta Ministry of Education, 32, 1–32.

Frisco Independent School District. (n.d.). *Future-ready learner.* https://www.friscoisd.org/about/future-ready/learner

Fry, R. (2023, December 18). *Fewer young men are in college, especially at 4-year schools.* Pew Research Center. https://www.pewresearch.org/short-reads/2023/12/18/fewer-young-men-are-in-college-especially-at-4-year-schools

G360 Surveys. (n.d.). *The five practices of leadership.* https://g360surveys.com/five-practices-of-exemplary-leadership

Gay, G. (2018). *Culturally responsive teaching: Theory, research, and practice.* Teachers College Press.

Gewertz, C. (2015, September 30). The Common Core explained. *Education Week.* https://www.edweek.org/teaching-learning/the-common-core-explained/2015/09

Gibbs, G. (1988). *Learning by doing: A guide to teaching and learning methods.* FEU.

Gillies, R. M., Ashman, A. F., & Terwel, J. (Eds.). (2008). *The teacher's role in implementing cooperative learning in the classroom.* Springer.

Graydin. (2022). *What is the Waterfall Effect?* https://www.graydin.com/blog/2022/01/11/2022-1-11-what-is-the-waterfall-effect

Grigoropoulos, J. E. (2021). Educational leadership: Cultivating leadership qualities generates student leaders. In M. D. Avgerinou & P. Pelonis (Eds.), *Handbook of research on k–12 blended and virtual learning through the i²Flex classroom model* (pp. 162–173). IGI Global.

Grisolía, C. M., & Serra, M. (2020). Effectiveness of praise-question-encourage (P-Q-E) commenting guidelines during teacher-written feedback on EFL learners' rewrites: A case study. In D. L. Banegas, M. De Stefani, P. Rebolledo, T. R. Troncoso, & R. Smith (Eds.), *Horizontes 1: ELT teacher-research in Latin America* (pp. 129–161). IATEFL. http://resig.weebly.com/uploads/2/6/3/6/26368747/horizontes_ebook.pdf

Guhlin, M. (2024, August 26). *TCEA ELEs: Essential learning expectations.* TCEA. https://blog.tcea.org/tcea-eles-essential-learning-expectations

Guidara, W. (2022). *Unreasonable hospitality.* Optimism Press.

Han, E. (2022a, January 18). *What is design thinking & why is it important?.* Harvard Business School Online. https://online.hbs.edu/blog/post/what-is-design-thinking

Han, E. (2022b, February 22). *5 examples of design thinking in business.* Harvard Business School Online. https://online.hbs.edu/blog/post/design-thinking-examples

Hancock, J. (n.d.). *Six thinking hats.* MindTools. https://www.mindtools.com/ajlpp1e/six-thinking-hats

Harry, B., & Klingner, J. (2014). *Why are so many minority students in special education?: Understanding race and disability in schools.* Teachers College Press.

Hattie, J., & Timperley, H. (2007). The power of feedback. *Review of Educational Research, 77*(1). 81–112. https://doi.org/10.3102/003465430298487

Hauwiller, J. (2019, February 19). The seven critical pillars of your personal brand. *Forbes*. https://www.forbes.com/sites/forbescoachescouncil/2019/02/19/the-seven-critical-pillars-of-your-personal-brand

Hehir, T., Grindal, T., Freeman, B., Lamoreau, R., Borquaye, Y., & Burke, S. (2016). *A summary of the evidence on inclusive education*. Abt Associates. https://files.eric.ed.gov/fulltext/ED596134.pdf

History.com Editors. (2024, February 27). *Brown v. Board of Education*. History. https://www.history.com/topics/black-history/brown-v-board-of-education-of-topeka

Hollings-Tennant, J. (2021, October 15). *6 dyslexic superpowers*. IDL Group. https://idlsgroup.com/news/6-dyslexic-superpowers

Hreha, J. (2023, July 26). *How to learn from failure using the entrepreneurial mindset*. Persona. https://www.personatalent.com/development/learn-from-failure

Johnston, W. (2024, April 22). *Many in Gen Z ditch colleges for trade schools. Meet the "toolbelt generation."* NPR. https://www.npr.org/2024/04/22/1245858737/gen-z-trade-vocational-schools-jobs-college

Jones, B., & Leverenz, C. (2017). Building personal brands with digital storytelling eportfolios. *International Journal of ePortfolio, 7*(1), 67–91.

Kane, D. (2023, October 10). Don't just tell students to solve problems. Teach them how. *UC San Diego Today.* https://today.ucsd.edu/story/dont-just-tell-students-to-solve-problems-teach-them-to

Karami, A. (2023, September 4). *Problem-solving and decision-making frameworks: Essential tools for UX design and product management*. LinkedIn. https://www.linkedin.com/pulse/problem-solving-decision-making-frameworks-essential-tools-karami

Kharbach, M. (2024, May 8). *Experiential learning simply explained*. Educators Technology. https://www.educatorstechnology.com/2023/08/experiential-learning.html

King, S. (2023, May 23). *Students leading the way*. SSAT. https://www.ssatuk.co.uk/blog/students-leading-the-way

Klein, A. (2024, January 22). National ed-tech plan outlines how schools can tackle 3 big digital inequities. *EducationWeek*. https://www.edweek.org/technology/national-ed-tech-plan-outlines-how-schools-can-tackle-3-big-digital-inequities/2024/01

Korthagen, F. A. (2001). *Linking practice and theory: The pedagogy of realistic teacher education*. Routledge.

Kouzes, J. M., & Posner, B. Z. (2024). *The student leadership challenge: Five practices for becoming an exemplary leader*. Wiley. https://www.google.co.uk/books/edition/_/l5D5EAAAQBAJ?hl=en&gbpv=0&kptab=overview

Kuratko, D. F. (2011). Entrepreneurship theory, process, and practice in the 21st century. *International Journal of Entrepreneurship and Small Business, 13*(1), 8–17.

Larmer, J., Mergendoller, J., & Boss, S. (2015). *Setting the standard for project-based learning*. ASCD.

Leadership in Action. (2015). *What are learning standards?* New England Secondary School Consortium. https://www.newenglandssc.org/wp-content/uploads/2015/12/NESSC_Briefing_No10.pdf

Leung, A., Fine, P. D., Blizard, R., Tonni, I., İlhan, D., & Louca, C. (2022). Teacher feedback and student learning—the students' perspective. *Journal of Dentistry, 125,* 104242.

Leverton, K. (2021, June 29). *Building student agency by collaborating on learning standards.* Edutopia. https://www.edutopia.org/article/building-student-agency-collaborating-learning-standards

LinkedIn. (2024). *What are the best digital tools to support student entrepreneurship?.* https://www.linkedin.com/advice/3/what-best-digital-tools-support-student-entrepreneurship-ayg6f#:~:text=For%20idea%20generation%2C%20students%20can,gather%20feedback%20from%20potential%20customers.

Marvin, H. (2024, January 29). Optimizing student check-ins: 5 must-have factors for effectiveness. *Satchel Pulse.* https://blog.teamsatchel.com/pulse/optimizing-student-check-ins-5-must-have-factors-for-effectiveness

Maryville University. (2020, May 28). *The evolution of social media: How did it begin, and where could it go next?* https://online.maryville.edu/blog/evolution-social-media

Masterson, V. (2023, May 1) *Future of jobs 2023: These are the most in-demand skills now - and beyond.* World Economic Forum. https://www.weforum.org/agenda/2023/05/future-of-jobs-2023-skills

Maxwell, J. C. (2014). *Good leaders ask great questions: Your foundation for successful leadership.* Center Street.

McGathey, L. (2018, February 18). Celina HS tech specialist, students keep district moving forward. *Celina Record.* https://starlocalmedia.com/celinarecord/news/celina-hs-tech-specialist-students-keep-district-moving-forward/article_12b22760-1401-11e8-a2b6-333aa8a440e3.html

McKibben, S. (2023, September 1). *When the obstacle is the way.* ASCD. https://www.ascd.org/el/articles/when-the-obstacle-is-the-way

McLeod, S. (2024, January 24). *Maslow's hierarchy of needs.* SimplyPsychology. https://www.simplypsychology.org/maslow.html

McMahon, K., Ruggeri, A., Kämmer, J. E., & Katsikopoulos, K. V. (2016). Beyond idea generation: The power of groups in developing ideas. *Creativity Research Journal, 28*(3), 247–257.

Mendoza, K. (2022, October 14). *Reflecting on over a decade of digital citizenship education.* Common Sense Media. https://www.commonsensemedia.org/kids-action/articles/reflecting-on-over-a-decade-of-digital-citizenship-education

Merriam-Webster. (n.d.). Entrepreneur. In Merriam-Webster.com dictionary. Retrieved December 14, 2024, from https://www.merriam-webster.com/dictionary/entrepreneur

Miller, J. (Host). (2020, September 24). Tisha Poncio & digital portfolios (No. 47) [Audio podcast episode]. In *EduDuctTape.* Jake Miller. http://jakemiller.net/eduducttape-episode-47

Minero, E. (2019, February 5). *10 powerful community-building ideas.* Edutopia. https://www.edutopia.org/article/10-powerful-community-building-ideas

Messier, N. (2022, April 15). *Authentic assessments*. Center for the Advancement of Teaching Excellence, University of Chicago. https://teaching.uic.edu/cate-teaching-guides/assessment-grading-practices/authentic-assessments

Meyer, A., Rose, D.H., & Gordon, D. (2014). *Universal design for learning: Theory and Practice*. CAST Professional Publishing.

Meyer, C. A. (1992). What's the difference between *authentic* and *performance* assessment. *Educational Leadership, 49*(8), 39–40. https://files.ascd.org/staticfiles/ascd/pdf/journals/ed_lead/el_199205_meyer.pdf

Mielke, C. (2023, September 1). *Reducing teacher workloads*. ASCD. https://www.ascd.org/el/articles/reducing-teacher-workloads

Miller, A. (2019, May 8). *Treating reflection as a habit, not an event*. Edutopia. https://www.edutopia.org/article/treating-reflection-habit-not-event

Mirel. J. (2006, June 22). The traditional high school. *Education Next, 6*(1). https://www.educationnext.org/the-traditional-high-school

National Association of Secondary School Principals. (2018). *Activity 5: Developing student leaders*. https://www.nassp.org/leading-success/module-1-developing-leadership-skills-for-change/activity-5-developing-student-leaders

National Center for Education Statistics. (2003). *Internet access in U.S. public schools and classrooms: 1994–2002*. U.S. Department of Education. https://nces.ed.gov/pubs2004/2004011.pdf

Neuman, M., & Simmons, W. (2000). Leadership for student learning. *Phi Delta Kappan, 82*(1), 9–12.

Ng, Z. J. (2024, June 25). *Helping students manage conflict*. Edutopia. https://www.edutopia.org/article/helping-students-manage-conflict

Nollmeyer, G., Weger, S., & Penrose, A. (2018, November 27). *Three before me*. Classroom management toolbox Eastern Washington University. https://inside.ewu.edu/managementtoolbox/three-before-me

Northern Illinois University Center for Innovative Teaching and Learning. (2012). Formative and summative assessment. In *Instructional guide for university faculty and teaching assistants*. https://www.niu.edu/citl/resources/guides/instructional-guide

Northouse, P. G. (2014). *Introduction to leadership: Concepts and practice*. Sage.

Pellegrino, J. W., & Hilton, M. L. (Eds.) (2012). *Education for life and work: Developing transferable knowledge and skills in the 21st century*. National Academies Press. https://nap.nationalacademies.org/read/13398/chapter/1

Plano Independent School District. (n.d.). *Portrait of a graduate*. https://www.pisd.edu/Page/15050

Poncio, T. (2021, February 24). *Why are digital portfolios powerful in a classroom?* Global EdTech. https://global-edtech.com/why-are-digital-portfolios-powerful-in-a-classroom

Poonvichaen, J., & Sutheejariyawat, P. (2022). Practicing collaborative teachers to strengthen student's visionary leadership skills. *Education Quarterly Reviews, 5*(3), 231–235.

PowerSchool (2023, November 16). *The PLC. handbook for educators: Unlocking professional learning communities.* https://www.powerschool.com/blog/plc-handbook

Prothero, A. (2024, April 3). Students think social media is fine, but teachers see a mental health minefield. *EducationWeek.* https://www.edweek.org/leadership/students-think-social-media-is-fine-but-teachers-see-a-mental-health-minefield/2024/03

Posner, B. Z. (2012). Effectively Measuring Student Leadership. Administrative Sciences, 2(4), 221–234. https://doi.org/10.3390/admsci2040221

Ramachandran, V. S. (2012). *Encyclopedia of human behavior.* Academic Press.

Rath, T. (2007). *StrengthsFinder 2.0.* Simon and Schuster.

Reigeluth, C. M., & An, Y. (2021). *Merging the instructional design process with learner-centered theory: The holistic 4D model.* Routledge.

Rogers, R. J. (2023, February 18). Learning journals: A powerful student feedback system. *Richard Rodgers: Decrypt, define, delineate.* https://richardjamesrogers.com/2018/02/18/learning-journals-a-powerful-student-feedback-system

Rose, J. (2012, May 9). How to break free of our 19th-century factory-model education system. *The Atlantic.* https://www.theatlantic.com/business/archive/2012/05/how-to-break-free-of-our-19th-century-factory-model-education-system/256881

Rosenshine, B., & Meister, C. (1994). Reciprocal teaching: A review of the research. *Review of Educational Research,* 64(4), 479–530.

Ruiz, D. M. (1997). *The four agreements: A practical guide to personal freedom.* Amber-Allen Publishing.

Ruman, H. (2024). *10 project-based learning (PBL) examples.* SmartLab. https://www.smartlablearning.com/project-based-learning-examples

Ryan, T., Henderson, M., & Phillips, M. (2019). Feedback modes matter: Comparing student perceptions of digital and non-digital feedback modes in higher education. *British Journal of Educational Technology,* 50(3), 1507–1523.

Saad, L. (2019, October 28). *Teachers who promote creativity see educational results.* Gallup. https://news.gallup.com/opinion/gallup/245600/teachers-promote-creativity-educational-results.aspx

Sanako Blog. (2024, January 22). *Peer-to-peer feedback - unlock the hidden power of your students.* https://sanako.com/peer-to-peer-feedback-unlock-the-hidden-power-of-your-students

Sawyer, K. (2019). *The creative classroom: Innovative teaching for 21st-century learners.* Teachers College Press.

Schleunes, K. A. (1979, December). Enlightenment, reform, reaction: The schooling revolution in Prussia. *Central European History,* 12(4), 315–342. https://doi.org/10.1017/S0008938900022457

Shaun. (2024). *How to throw darts with precision.* DartHelp. https://darthelp.com/guides/how-to-throw-darts

Shemshack, A., & Spector, J. M. (2020, October 23). A systematic literature review of personalized learning terms. *Smart Learning Environments,* 7(1), 33. https://doi.org/10.1186/s40561-020-00140-9

Staake, J. (2024, February 12). *Formative, summative, and more types of assessments for education.* We Are Teachers. https://www.weareteachers.com/types-of-assessments

Stanford, L. (2023, December 11). More states are creating a "portrait of a graduate." Here's why. *EducationWeek.* https://www.edweek.org/policy-politics/more-states-are-creating-a-portrait-of-a-graduate-heres-why/2023/12

Strong, R., Wynn, J. T., Irby, T. L., & Lindner, J. R. (2013). The relationship between students' leadership style and self-directed learning level. *Journal of Agricultural Education, 54*(20), 174–185. https://eric.ed.gov/?id=EJ1122375.

Students Who Advocate Technology. (Host). (2021, February 21). Digital portfolios (No. 4) [Audio podcast episode]. In *SWATIFY.* https://open.spotify.com/episode/3kSTfwMpViiFBFeJ6UGydB

Teachers of Tomorrow (2024, April 8). *Teacher shortages in the U.S.: Challenges, solutions & initiatives in 2024.* https://www.teachersoftomorrow.org/blog/insights/teacher-shortages-in-the-us

Texas Education Agency. (2011). Chapter 1: Historical overview of assessment in Texas. *Technical Digest 2010–2011.* https://teadev.tea.texas.gov/sites/default/files/digest11-chap01.pdf

Texas Education Agency. (2021, November 19). *Chapter 112. Texas essential knowledge and skills for science: Subchapter b. middle school.* https://tea.texas.gov/academics/curriculum-standards/teks-review/112b-twowith-header.pdf

Todăriță, E. T. (2021, July 11). Leadership style determination according to Robert Blake and Jane Mouton's Managerial Grid. *International Conference KNOWLEDGE-BASED ORGANIZATION, 27*(1), 241–246. https://doi.org/10.2478/kbo-2021-0037

Topping, K. J. (2005, December). Trends in peer learning. *Educational Psychology, 25*(6), 631–645. https://doi.org/10.1080/01443410500345172

Tomlinson, C. A. (2001). *How to differentiate instruction in mixed-ability classrooms.* ASCD.

Unin, N., & Bearing, P. (2016, June 15). Brainstorming as a way to approach student-centered learning in the ESL classroom. *Procedia-Social and Behavioral Sciences, 224,* 605–612. https://doi.org/10.1016/j.sbspro.2016.05.450

University of Connecticut. (n.d.) *Reflections.* https://edtech.uconn.edu/portfolios/reflections/#:~:text=Reflection%20is%20a%20meaning%2Dmaking,the%20progress%20of%20the%20individual

Watters, A. (2015, April 25). The invented history of 'the factory model of education.' *Hack Education.* https://hackeducation.com/2015/04/25/factory-model

Weider, L. (n.d.). *The N.E.A. Committee of Ten.* University of Notre Dame. https://www3.nd.edu/~rbarger/www7/neacom10.html

Wells, R. (2024, January 22). 8 high-income skills to learn in 2024. *Forbes.* https://www.forbes.com/sites/rachelwells/2024/01/22/8-high-income-skills-to-learn-in-2024/?sh=33f6b460138.

Whiting, K. (2020, October 21).*These are the top 10 job skills of tomorrow – and how long it takes to learn them.* World Economic Forum. https://www.weforum.org/agenda/2020/10/top-10-work-skills-of-tomorrow-how-long-it-takes-to-learn-them

Winston, B. E., & Patterson, K. (2006). An integrative definition of leadership. *International Journal of Leadership Studies*, *1*(2), 6–66.

World Population Review. (n.d.). *Common Core states 2024*. https://worldpopulationreview.com/state-rankings/common-core-states

Yan, Z., & Carless, D. (2021). Self-assessment is about more than self: the enabling role of feedback literacy. *Assessment & Evaluation in Higher Education*, *47*(7), 1116–1128. https://doi.org/10.1080/02602938.2021.2001431

Zaabalawi, R. S., & Zaabalawi, J. (2024, July 19). Portfolios versus exams: A study to gauge the better student assessment tool. *Language Testing in Asia* 14, 28. https://doi.org/10.1186/s40468-024-00296-y

Index

www.ingramcontent.com/pod-product-compliance
Lightning Source LLC
Chambersburg PA
CBHW081534120626
46550CB00009B/2720

* 9 7 9 8 8 8 8 3 7 0 4 7 6 *